How to Say 'No' and Mean It

How to Say 'No' and Mean It

Survival Skills For Parents

Karen Sullivan

INDEX

This edition published 2005 for
Index Books Limited

Thorsons
An Imprint of HarperCollins*Publishers*
77–85 Fulham Palace Road,
Hammersmith, London W6 8JB

The website address is: www.thorsonselement.com

and *Thorsons* are trademarks of
HarperCollins*Publishers* Ltd

Published by Thorsons 2003

10 9 8 7 6 5 4 3 2

Cartoons by Harry Venning

A catalogue record of this book is
available from the British Library

ISBN 0 00 774198 7

Printed and bound in Great Britain by
Clays Ltd, St Ives plc

For Max, with all my love

Contents

Part Two: Discipline in Action!

Introduction

Never before has discipline been such an apparent problem in our society. Teachers complain of the impossibility of maintaining classroom control with increasingly delinquent pupils. Many parents feel overwhelmed by children who appear to show little regard for rules and acceptable behaviour. Even more worrying, lawlessness is rife among children. In fact, a recent poll by the Youth Justice Board in the UK found that one in four children admitted to committing a crime in the last year. The most common crimes were fare-dodging, shoplifting, graffiti, criminal damage and carrying a weapon. One in five also admitted stealing from school, handling stolen goods or stealing from home.

The blame for the slide appears to shift between parents and teachers, with no one taking real responsibility. The result is, of course, that no one does.

I believe that discipline is firmly rooted in the home. Teachers and schools have a responsibility, too, but their role is more one of maintenance and reinforcement. This is because discipline is not about controlling children, or laying down the law. It's about guiding children to adulthood, and investing them with respect for themselves and others. Indeed, giving our children self-respect is the linchpin to any healthy discipline policy and the key to empowering our children to make the right choices in life. One of the most important jobs a parent has is to teach life lessons to their child, and behaviour is part of that. For people to live together in harmony, there has to be a basic level of respect for others.

All children need discipline. It defines their world, and makes it a safe place to live. They know their boundaries and they can express themselves and show some independence within them. Children without discipline are effectively thrust into the world without a guide, and they are forced to make decisions and choices that they are not equipped to make. There is a curious divide between the way modern parents approach discipline. Many children are left to their own devices for long periods of time and expected to behave in an adult fashion, literally looking after themselves. These children have far too much freedom, without the guidance they need to use it healthily and successfully. On the other hand, however, some children are expected to behave beautifully at all times, and to achieve and succeed. With no personal freedom, these children are over-disciplined, with equally disastrous results.

The best parents are those who allow their children some free rein, some scope to be children, some freedom to be themselves, while still respecting the rights and needs of others. What children need is guidance, and an understanding of the world around them. This requires time and patience. Constant explanations are required to give children a realistic reason for why certain behaviours are unacceptable or disrespectful. They need to be taught the impact of the way they behave on other people. Parents must teach them to communicate, negotiate, compromise, make decisions, make choices, develop self-control, be themselves and take pride in who they are. When they are taught these lessons in the context of an unconditionally loving home, they learn to live happily with other people.

Parents represent the first relationships our children have in their lives. These relationships must be healthy and built on the sound principles of love, respect, care, nurturing, guidance, acceptance, understanding, communication, mutual expression and, above all, security. Most of what our children do in their lives revolves around relationships and interactions – with friends, classmates, teachers, coaches, other family members, peers, baby-sitters, carers and virtually every other person with whom they come into contact. If they learn the lessons of healthy relationships and the ability to interact early on, they will be given the tools they need to find their place in the world.

What all parents need to do is provide their child with an understanding of how other people feel and think, and what will be expected of them in certain situations. No child knows instinctively how to behave, and with even the best guidance, there will always be times when emotion overtakes logic, or exuberance overtakes wisdom, or temper overtakes self-control. And this is where patience comes in.

Patience is sometimes in short supply in today's hectic lifestyles. Stress is a significant problem and impacts both on the time we have to spend with our children and on the way we are able to interact with them. No one can exhibit patience when they feel exhausted, tired, fed up and powerless, and this has a dramatic effect on the way our children learn to see themselves. Our expectations tend to be high because we take our parenting responsibilities seriously, and often see any rebellion or bad behaviour as a reflection of our poor parenting skills. We often lose a lot of the joy of parenting because we become overly caught up in the role of disciplinarian. And with that, we misplace our sense of humour, which is one of the best tools we have to negotiate the parenting minefield.

We do not let our children be children: we control rather than teach; we expect adult behaviour and decision-making in children who have little resources or understanding of what is expected; we punish and penalize rather than focus on the very good things that are happening around us. The end result is that many children feel powerless, valueless, disrespected and unloved. They develop poor self-identities and never acquire the self-respect required for them to be confident, conscious and caring members of society.

On the other hand, the overemphasis on self-esteem in the past few years has caused parents to nurture their children too much (*see page 68*), allowing them to get away with completely unacceptable behaviour in the belief that they have the right to express themselves and their unique characteristics. The result of this is, of course, that children become tyrants and expect the world to bow to them. This is unhealthy for many reasons, but in terms of discipline, its impact is significant. Over-pampered children have no respect for anyone else and feel that they have a divine right to have their needs met. Not only is this a dangerous viewpoint because children tend to believe that they are 'above' or 'better than' others and accepted rules, but they never actually develop self-respect. It's all too easy. Respect is earned (*see page 68*). Once again, a child who is not invested with self-respect will never fully understand the concept of discipline and accepted codes of behaviour.

Let me make one thing clear. This isn't necessarily the fault of parents, who almost always have good intentions and the best interests of their children at heart. Some of the problem is societal, where mutual respect is underplayed in so many areas of life. Parents are also under huge pressure of time, and simply do not have the resources to be full-time parents. Extended families tend to be far removed, so the benefit of wisdom handed down the generations is absent, and many parents have to rely on full-time carers to do their job for them. It's also difficult to be consistent when your resources are low and you need a little peace. Most importantly, children do not come with a manual, so many parents seek them out, and the amount of confusing information out there is positively criminal. It's not surprising that many parents feel out of their depth and unsure of how to deal effectively with their children.

What tends to happen is a descent into what one Canadian doctor terms the 'talk, persuade, argue, yell, hit' syndrome, in which all attempts to negotiate behaviour end with the same result – an almighty row and possibly violence born out of sheer frustration. No parent feels good interacting with their children on this level. Children may be small and necessarily inferior on many levels, but this inferiority is something that rankles, and they want and demand a little power and respect. You think you are in control; they think they ought to be. The end result is locked horns, a power struggle and, ultimately, chaos. No one wins in these situations, and everyone goes away with bad feelings: guilt, frustration, anger, powerlessness and the lurking suspicions that they have no control over their lives.

When I became a football coach to 12 unruly little boys, I saw my role as showing them how to develop their skills and play better football. I pointed out (constantly) the things they were doing wrong, and showed them a better way. This was a steep learning curve for me. What I ended up with was not better footballers, but a disgruntled, frustrated bunch of boys who lost their belief in themselves. Their behaviour began to decline and they lost their enthusiasm. It occurred to me suddenly that all children, regardless of their situation, need to feel good about themselves and that the best way to do that was to focus on the good things they did – as well as their effort and attitude. I changed my policy and did just that – praising good moves, passing and team spirit. Teaching them took on a new meaning. When they felt confident, they were more likely to listen to constructive criticism and take on board the techniques and tactics. Morale improved as did team spirit and overall behaviour, and at the time of writing our team is top of their division.

I'd always approached the upbringing of my two boys in this way, but I hadn't made the connection that all children require the same treatment and care. And the results are dramatic and quickly realized. We get the most from our children, and instil in them a sense of pride and self-respect, when we respect them and their efforts. Whether it's learned behaviour or behaving to attain the reward of attention and praise is irrelevant. The fact is that children learn to feel good about themselves, feel good about the way their behaviour is perceived and accepted, and thereby continue the behaviour. What more could you want?

There are many tried and tested techniques for disciplining positively and helping our children to adapt to their role in society. All children are different and require slightly altered approaches to daily discipline. However, the philosophy underpinning the techniques outlined in this book are suitable for all children, because they celebrate uniqueness, they are built on love and understanding, and they focus on the key element of discipline: respect. Whether you have an ebullient toddler, a shy pre-schooler, a sulky teen or a seemingly uncontrollable pre-teen, these techniques will work, largely because there isn't a template set to negotiate all problem behaviours.

To get the most from this book, I recommend that you read all of Part One, which outlines how the philosophy works. It's very simple, really, and a good read is all that is required. With these tools and techniques under your hat, you may not even need to read Part Two, but it's there to dip into when problems arise. The second part concentrates on how to discourage behaviour that you don't want to see, and encourage what you *do*. In the end, the aim is family harmony and happy children with a healthy respect for others. And it works both in the short and long term.

This book will help if you have lost confidence in your ability to discipline your children, are struggling with the daily grind of keeping them on the straight and narrow, have problems communicating and getting your ideas across, feel that your children do not hear you, or even have difficulty getting your children to understand the concept of the word 'no' (a big problem, hence the title of this book). You'll find in this book all the tools, tips and techniques you need to bring about great change in both the way your children behave and see themselves, and in the way they interact with others and look upon the world in general. Start now, and watch your family dynamic transform.

Part One

Terms, Techniques and Tools

Active Listening

How well do you listen to your children? Ask yourself honestly. Are you busy reading the paper, cooking or thinking through a business proposal when they chat to you? Do you think that the occasional nod or 'hmm' will be sufficient to show your interest?

Children twig easily when they do not have their parents' full attention, hence the commonly heard cry: 'You aren't listening!' or 'I just told you that!' And when they do not manage to get the attention they require through verbal communication, they will be determined to get it in other ways. A great deal of disruptive or 'naughty' behaviour is undertaken simply to get some attention. If a child learns that being good and quiet gets them nowhere, you can bet they will raise a bit of a ruckus – largely because it always works. Even angry words and punishments are better than nothing.

Active listening is an important tool for all parents. It involves:

- hearing what your child has to say, both in terms of the words he is using and the feelings between the words
- asking questions
- providing a real response to questions
- offering words to help your child explain the way he is feeling
- giving him a non-judgmental sounding board for thoughts, ideas and emotions

Children feel more secure when they can express themselves and know that what they are feeling is acceptable. They feel validated when they are given a respectful audience.

In a nutshell, active listening is a way of talking to someone with sympathy or empathy. It is respectful of your child's thoughts and feelings because you don't just sit there – you attempt to see the world through the eyes of your child. What's more, you suspend your judgment and your opinions for the duration of the conversation and commit yourself to understanding how your child sees or saw a situation. This doesn't mean you have to agree, but you do need to show willing.

In many cases, problem behaviours can be stamped out when parents are able to see and hear issues affecting their children's wellbeing. A rambling story, during which the average parent might tune out, can hold a multitude of clues into a child's emotional state. Giving words to problems and feelings, identifying potential issues, showing love and acceptance, and encouraging your child to express himself all help to build self-respect. More importantly, however, children learn the value of listening themselves, a tool which will empower them in many difficult situations. They will also learn to return the respect shown to them by listening to you.

Active listening has two main goals:

1   to understand what your child is thinking, from his or her point of view
2   to communicate back and check your understanding with the child

You become an active participant in the conversation. It can be difficult to do this at times, particularly when you are annoyed about behaviour, disagree fundamentally with what your child is saying or you are very busy. But it's worth the effort. Put yourself in the right frame of mind. Tell yourself that you will not only *listen* but you will *hear* your child, no matter what. Use non-judgmental questions to keep the conversation going. Avoid anything confrontational. The point is to show understanding.

Sometimes all that is required is a quiet audience, with gentle reassurance or questions at the right moments. As long as your child feels that he is being heard, you have established the type of communication that precludes serious and long-term behavioural problems.

Apologies

Should children apologize? Should we?

Parents often behave in exactly the way they discourage their children from behaving. We shout, argue, lose our patience and even use physical violence, in the form of smacking, for example. Yet very few parents are willing to take responsibility for their actions and apologize for unacceptable behaviour. Is it not surprising, then, that children are confused about expectations, feel a (rightful) sense of injustice and double standards, and a lack of respect?

Providing a Positive Example

Parents, like children, need to learn to apologize when they break rules and when they make mistakes. One of the problems facing society today is that children tend to feel no sense of responsibility and believe that rules or laws are not applicable to them. It's easy to see the root of this ideology, as they often grow up surrounded by a series of double standards, none of which is explained or justified.

When we apologize to our children, we admit that we have made a mistake, that we are human. Mistakes *are* human and it is through these mistakes that we learn and grow. If we are unable to admit ours, our children will learn to hide theirs, which keeps them isolated and creates a fear of discovery. This not only undermines communication between parent and child (and all other authority figures), but prevents children from taking responsibility for their own actions – a fundamental component of respect and self-respect.

Children also need to be encouraged to admit mistakes, to learn that people are often very forgiving when they attempt to make amends. From about the age of four, children can understand the concept of 'I'm sorry'. When we apologize to our children, we need to explain our feelings before and after, in order to repair the damage and provide a positive example. We do so with an expectation of forgiveness. If we do not offer the same gift to our children, they will learn nothing. Everyone, children and adults alike, is entitled to bad moods and the odd occurrence of poor behaviour. The purpose of apology is to show that you see where the inappropriate action lies and to find a way to avoid it in the future. It opens interaction and heals relationships.

Avoiding Labels

It's easy to label children and most of us do it from the day they are born – and sometimes even before that. I've heard parents actually say that their child was 'easy' until he was born; in other words, a good pregnancy or the opposite can lead a parent to label a child before he has seen his first light. A poor sleeper, a fussy eater, 'good', 'clingy', 'difficult' – these are all labels that help parents to explain and define their children's characteristics from a very early age. It is a trend that continues throughout toddlerhood and well into the teen years. The problem is that labels end up becoming self-fulfilling prophecies. Here's why.

When a child is born, he trusts his parents completely. He asks questions about his world, and they are answered. Parents are the all-powerful source of knowledge, and

children learn by watching and listening. They are told that the sky is blue. They are told that 1, 2, 3 is counting. It is pointed out that shoes go on feet, and that night-time is for sleeping. They are told that cats have kittens, that books are for reading, that a cow says 'moo'.

Children believe what they are told, and this belief is validated by the fact that the outside world seems to be in agreement. Grandparents give the same response to questions; nursery school colleagues all believe the same thing; a baby-sitter confirms that cows do say 'moo'. Their trust is complete. Everything that is said to a child will be taken seriously. Children believe what they are told.

Today's parents are busy, tired and often unaware that the little things they say can have a profound impact. In sheer frustration, we may call our children stupid, naughty, bad, spoiled, silly, jealous, dumb, impossible to live with, selfish, self-centred ... all sorts of things that slip out in the course of an argument, or in the throes of a chaotic day. When parents become angry, upset, frustrated, busy or just exhausted, they often say things they don't intend. This is, of course, the source of much parental guilt.

But these words and throwaway comments can have deep-seated ramifications. Children believe their parents implicitly, and if you tell them they are stupid, selfish or naughty, even in a burst of anger, they will have mentally filed that away. Every negative word that is used to define them will have been taken on board, even unconsciously. Children are not likely to remember the specific incident, nor will they be traumatized for life by being called impossible or horrid, but these experiences will have formed faulty bricks in the foundation of their self-image. When they are used repeatedly, these descriptions become labels, and labels have the habit of becoming a reality in terms of your children's behaviour.

The Danger of Positive Labels

But even positive labels can have a damaging effect on children. Going too far in the other direction, and over-focusing on the positive aspects of your child's personality or talents, can become a cross to bear. Constantly being labelled bright, musical, good or funny is very flattering, and all children will benefit from praise and the good feelings that go with it. However, when the same terms are used repeatedly, a child starts to believe the press and even minor setbacks can throw his self-image into doubt. Furthermore, they may try too hard to live up to imposs- ible expectations, which can ultimately lead to rebellion and a poor self-identity.

Labels have no place in a loving relationship. No human being is simple enough to be categorized with one or more adjectives, and because children believe what they are told they tend then to act according to the labels they are given.

You may think that labelling a child 'good' will, therefore, lead to good behaviour, and in the short term you may be right. But in the long term, you are teaching your child nothing about himself. An important part of parenting involves encouraging children to like and accept themselves for who they are. In this way, they develop self-respect, and respect for others. If they spend their childhoods living up to labels, they have learned nothing about themselves.

In short, avoid labels of any sort.

Being Unique

All children are different and their individual character-istics should be celebrated and constantly taken into consideration. It's important to remember that many of the qualities we tend to suppress in our children, such as dogged determination, pride, exuberance, high energy, constant negotiation and a sense of fun, are the very characteristics we value greatly in adulthood.

Many parents expect all children to behave in a similar fashion, and this is where much discipline goes wrong. A quiet, introspective child should never be disciplined in the same way as one who is effervescent and outgoing. Nor should we expect their behaviour to be the same. The qualities that combine to make our children who they are should be nurtured and respected. Trying to quash the spirit of a lively pre-schooler will not only be impossible, but you run the risk of ruining his self-image in the process. He'll learn that it is not acceptable to be himself, and although he might change his behaviour to please you, he will feel confused about who he is. In this type of scenario, parents need to learn to channel energy within acceptable boundaries, rather than trying to force a child into a mould he will never fit.

Tailor Discipline to Your Child's Personality

Every child has different strengths and weaknesses. Although it is a time-consuming process, particularly for parents with more than one child, it is important that these are recognized and celebrated. Too much of the discipline of today appears to be aimed at helping our children to *conform*: a highly strung child needs to be calmed; a quiet child needs to be brought out; a poor student needs to concentrate; an academic needs music lessons or extracurricular sports to round him out. It's not surprising that children then lash out and rebel. If we were expected, day in and day out, to be someone we were not, chances are that we would respond in exactly the same way – with frustration.

A lively child should not be 'controlled', but taught appropriate behaviour in various situations. A shy child should not be expected to hold a long eye-to-eye conversation with an adult, but he can be taught to be polite. Look at the unique qualities of your children and help them to feel proud of who they are. Self-pride is one of the most important aspects of self-respect and self-liking. And children who like themselves have little need to behave in ways that are completely unacceptable.

Birth Order

There's no question that birth order plays a part in a child's defining characteristics, and it also affects the way we deal with our children. We tend to be harder on the first-born, in an attempt, perhaps, to 'get it right', often through uncertainty and not a little experimentation. We tend to relax the rules through the ranks, which can lead not only to problems with sibling rivalry, but also identity.

A great deal of research has gone into understanding

how birth order affects a child's personality and outlook on life, and it's worth bearing this in mind when considering the expectations you have for your children.

In recent research, Frank Sulloway, Ph.D., of Stanford University's Center for Advanced Study in the Behavioral Sciences, found that the eldest child is twice as likely as a younger sibling to become a top company executive (in other words, successful). First-borns tend to identify with their parents, align with authority and support the status quo. Later-borns are more likely to become rebels. They're probably more adventurous and less conventional, says Sulloway, since they're often forced as kids to explore new territory in order to compete with older siblings. He also points out that siblings have to be seen in the context of their family: an eldest child might seem rebellious, but is actually quite conservative when compared with his younger siblings.

First-borns

Eldest children are the ground-breakers – first to be born, first to be potty-trained, first to attend school, first to their parents' affections. Their milestones are celebrated, their development charted, their shortcomings the subject of huge concern – in essence, they live their lives under a microscope and quickly learn what is expected of them. They have the benefit of more attention and praise – spending longer 'in the sun' than their siblings – but this does have drawbacks. Ironically, their very success often leads to anxiety: if being special hinges on performing to high standards, failure becomes increasingly significant. To protect against this disaster, many first-born children set even higher standards for themselves than their parents do and, as a result, are rarely satisfied. Any success they achieve is not enough. Over and over, they must prove they are not the failures they fear they might be. In terms of behaviour, this often manifests itself as behaving according to expectations, rather than developing a sense of the world around them and finding their own identities. There will be swings between being the 'good' child and probably roaring tantrums and periods of huge frustration when they find it all too much to bear.

First children are also in the unique position of having to give up being the sole focus of their parents' attention. This can lead to attention-seeking behaviour and a deep-seated feeling that they have been supplanted in their parents' affection. Jealousy, guilt and anger are normal feelings in an eldest child. Some children respond aggressively to their siblings; others become even more determined to behave well in order to protect their status. Most show a combination of both behaviours, helping feed the baby one moment, pinching her the next.

The upside is that they develop a sense of responsibility, being helpers, baby-sitters and mentors. The downside is that they tend to be bossy, expect others to listen to them and try to dominate every situation. As a parent, you should be aware of the need for your first-born to be treated as a child, not just a little adult helper. Allow him his moods and the other normal behaviours of childhood. Don't expect excellence, even if he is capable of it, because you'll only provide him with more cause for anxiety and stress, which will manifest itself in problem behaviours. Good enough is enough some of the time, and your child needs to feel that his strengths are recognized and his weaknesses accepted.

Middle Children

Those born in the middle of a family tend to feel that they aren't particularly significant – not the biggest and best, nor the cherished 'baby'. For this reason, middle children tend to rebel and find ways to get attention – any attention

– in order to lose their self-believed cloak of invisibility. Because their place within the family is less defined, they tend to have a wider circle of friends and depend more upon their peers for approval and a sense of power. It goes without saying that this can have a dramatic impact on behaviour, if parents are not quick to intervene before a child is led astray.

Parents tend not to impose the same high expectations on middle children, which allows them a certain amount of freedom to explore their individuality. However, many middle children feel less loved than their siblings, with fewer milestones marked, less parental angst about new situations and a far less proactive brand of parenting. This does not, of course, mean that middle children are less loved; it's simply that the majority of parents could never find the time or energy to maintain the intense interest a first child inspires, and they naturally become more relaxed.

In terms of behaviour, however, middle children do find they can get away with a lot more than their eldest siblings, and they are normally not afraid to try. They tend to choose a different path to older siblings, in order to avoid competition and to increase their chances of standing out and being noticed. And because they are so often the underdog, they will learn some important lessons, such as the art of negotiation, cooperation and even empathy. First-born children tend to be self-centred, while middle children often take a real interest in getting to know and understand others. But within the family unit, middle children often feel powerless and depend upon parental intervention, having little faith in themselves to sort out a problem.

This can lead to serious problems with the family dynamic as parents become frustrated by the constant demands for help, and embroiled in the centre of yet another battle. Middle children need to learn to trust and believe in their own worth, and to become confident enough to sort out their own disagreements. Parents need to learn to offer genuine praise for the middle child's unique abilities and qualities, and ensure that they are noticed and respected for who they are. In many families, the middle child is the 'stirrer'. A little time spent offering extra attention, helping him to feel important within the family, and ensuring that he knows it is acceptable to choose and follow his own path, will all help to relieve attention-seeking behaviour. This ensures that essential communication channels are in place, so that peers become less instrumental in your child's choices.

Youngest Children

Being the baby has both disadvantages and advantages. Youngest children tend to be fussed over and manage to get away with behaviour that older children can't, which can cause a certain amount of discontent in the ranks. However, they do tend to be overlooked as responsible individuals, and do not normally garner the respect they feel they deserve – and which they ultimately require.

Youngest children are normally parented in one of two ways: too much or too little. Some parents look upon their youngest as a chance to get everything right. With a little experience under their belts, they are determined to produce the perfect child. This can be an intolerable pressure for a child, with expectations that match or exceed those accorded to the eldest child. Other parents choose a different route, noting that their parenting has been largely successful with previous children and choosing, therefore, to take a more laid-back approach the last time round. It may also be that they simply do not have time to offer the same hands-on approach the others were given. These parents tend to give in more easily, to keep the youngest happy and content.

In the first case, children will respond in much the same way as first-born children, but will probably be more prone to tantrums because they do not feel the same need for parental approval that first-borns normally do. In the second case, children are likely to become used to having things their own way, with little parental intervention, and find it difficult to conform to expectations – at home, at school or in society at large. They may also become little princes or princesses, used to people bending over backwards to fulfil their every need.

In both cases, a youngest child may feel slightly disconnected. There is more emotional distance than between the first-born child and parents, and a more relaxed approach to parenting – however well intended – may have the effect of making a child feel slightly less loved and important.

It's important that these potential scenarios are recognized, and that your youngest child is given a specific role and highlighted place within the family. She should be given:

- responsibilities
- attention
- genuine praise for accomplishments
- her fair share of rules and realistic expectations

Children feel most secure when they are given boundaries, and even if you are fairly confident of your parenting skills, it's important to realize that a child does not know what to expect if you don't spell it out. It's often difficult for younger children to grow up in the shadow of their older siblings, and their unique characteristics must be noticed and accepted with the same interest and alacrity as for the older children. Being the baby may encourage some children to develop an uncanny ability to charm, so beware of being lured into situations you would normally find unacceptable.

The birth order debate is interesting and can help many parents understand their children's tendencies and patterns of behaviour. It's important to remember, however, that all families and family dynamics are different, and each child must be treated as an individual.

Choices

This is one of the key techniques for successful discipline, and prevents the horns-locked scenarios that regularly occur between parent and child. This technique involves offering choices, rather than giving instructions, laying down the law or ruling by overly authoritarian means. It provides children with a sense of power, which is crucial to personal development.

As adults, we all understand how it feels to be powerless, backed into a corner, perhaps by a dictatorial boss, financial circumstances or even too little time. How do we react? Normally with frustration, anger or apathy. Why, then, do we expect our children to react differently when they are robbed of any sense of power?

Life is about making choices – the right choices – and learning what happens when we choose the wrong direction. This is the essence of discipline: teaching our children to choose appropriate behaviour and action. In order for children to learn the art of decision-making, they need to be given choices regularly.

Offering choices does not mean allowing rules to fly out the window. Quite the opposite. It involves giving some scope for personal decisions within the structure of family rules and expectations. It gives children some control over their environment and behaviour, and teaches them that there are consequences to their actions. Here's how it works in practice.

Decision-making in Practice

Allow him to choose the way he behaves. In the middle of a temper tantrum, for example, offer a choice: 'You can stop shouting and screaming now, and I will be able to finish the shopping and we'll have time for a trip to the library. You can continue to shout and scream, I will be cross, and we will be too late to do anything other than go home. Which do you choose?' Give your child time to think and then respond accordingly. Whatever you do, be consistent. If you say that you won't have time for the library, don't go. If you say that you will, you must make the trip.

For an older child, this method works in a variety of situations:

- 'If you do your homework now, you can watch 20 minutes of television after dinner. If you don't do it now, you will have to go to bed straight after dinner'
- 'If you come home at 10pm after your party, I will trust you and allow you to go to the movies on your own on Saturday. If you don't come home on time, I will not be able to trust you on your own'

Whatever the situation, give a choice and let your child know the consequences of either one.

This technique works beautifully in situations that tend to end in tears. For example, 'Please get dressed now' is likely to be met with a firm 'no', as is 'Clean your room', 'Take out the rubbish', and even 'Be home before midnight'. It's much easier to approach things with an element of choice. Such as: 'Would you like to wear your pink tights and turtleneck, or the blue fleece with the flowers?' There is no question of your child not getting dressed, but she is involved in the decision-making process and feels empowered. Similarly, 'Do you want to clean your room tonight or shall we do it together on Saturday?', or 'Do you want to come in at 10 and watch a movie with me, or will I expect you some time before 12?' – both scenarios work much better than an order that is bound to be met with resistance.

This technique works even for small children, who soon learn that if they make a choice for short-term gain or attention, they may lose out on an expected treat or reward. Older children feel they are involved in the way their own lives are run. In all cases, a child feels in control of his situation, and is much more likely to behave appropriately, having made the choice himself.

Consistency

If there's one area where parents go wrong, it's here. Even with the best will in the world, parents become worn down by children – their negotiations, pleading, tantrums, tears and dogmatic approach to almost anything that arises. It's not surprising that we give in and allow the rules to slip, or a penalty to be relaxed, just to gain a little all-important peace.

But one slip and you've planted a seed in your child's mind: they gave in once and they'll do it again. You can bet that the next tantrum or howl will be longer and more determined because they know that they will, in the end, get their way. Moreover, where there is no consistency in discipline within a family, children feel slightly out of sorts and less secure. Without the boundaries that rules and discipline create, they can experience moments of fear and this is when they test and test those boundaries to make sure they are still there.

We often see this type of behaviour in families who have split up. One parent carries on the routine and usual discipline techniques; the other tries to make up for feelings of guilt or simply wants to keep the peace, thereby allowing the rules to slip. The children involved feel unbalanced and unsure. They produce all sorts of unacceptable patterns of behaviour in order to get a reaction, and to see how far they can push before those boundaries fall back into place. The disciplinarian parent tends to get the worst of it, because the children feel more secure in that environment and more able to lash out with a trusted and known entity.

The bottom line is that consistency produces results. If children know where they stand, they are less likely to behave badly. If they know you mean business when you impose a penalty or make a decision, they will learn that the actions that led to this situation are probably unacceptable and to be avoided in future. Consistency also involves imposing the same rules for all members of the family, and taking responsibility when any are broken. There's nothing better to engender a sense of injustice than different rules for different children. Make the rules, stick to them, and unless a well-reasoned argument proves them to be wrong, do not give in.

This does not, by any means, rob a child of space to be himself or to make choices. All of the tools in this book work best with a consistent approach to discipline. This creates boundaries in which a child – any child – will flourish.

Teachers

There are few techniques in this book that do not work well in the classroom. Stars and dots, for example, can be implemented on both an individual and a class basis. Two hundred dots can mean a class party or an afternoon of games and videos. A certain number of personal dots or stars can mean a much-coveted certificate. All of the techniques can be adapted to larger groups of children. Again, set out your expectations. Set out some class rules – all of which should be written inside the homework diary or something similar, and written in large letters and posted on the wall.

There will always be unruly members of the class who fail to respect your rules, but stay firm. Stick to pre-arranged penalties, use the yellow and red cards for warnings, and make it clear that you will not succumb to aggression, anger, taunting or any other form of unacceptable behaviour. This method also maintains the dignity of the children in the classroom, as shouting and manhandling simply do not need to take place.

Have a kick-off conversation or meeting with the children on the first day or two of school. It might help to put them into small groups to discuss the rules they think need to be maintained. Ask each group to present their ideas and write them on the blackboard. Have the class vote on the most important rules; add a few of your own (in line with your expectations), and then move on to rewards. Ask them what they'd like to work towards – what treats they'd like to see. Maybe a night off homework? A class party or trip? Some games or an extra-long break? Make sure that you find a series of rewards – both long-term and short-term – that will appeal to all children, not just a select few.

Similarly, ask the children to choose the penalties – time-out in a corner (behind a curtained-off area, and not in full view of the rest of the class), a trip to see the headmaster or the withdrawal of privileges, such as going outside for break time or going to the library.

Individual dots or stars can be awarded for good behaviour, effort, achievement or anything else you want to encourage within the classroom. Acts of kindness or helpfulness are good behaviours to encourage. Take time to praise the more difficult children for the good things they manage, even if they are falling down on the most basic elements of self-control or even achievement. If they feel they are good at something, they will be inspired to try their hand at other things.

Ignore the bad behaviour as much as possible before reaching for that yellow card. Riotous children can end up taking up all of your lesson time by provoking you to discipline them. Focus on their good behaviour and praise whatever you can, turning a blind eye to minor time-wasting indiscretions as much as possible. As long as you are consistent and do not bend the rules, even the most undisciplined child will learn that it's a waste of time trying to distract you from your purpose.

Help the children to develop a certain level of emotional expression. This not only helps them to understand their peers and the ramifications of unacceptable behaviour, but it helps to establish a good level of communication between you, which will keep things on an even keel. Many children will simply not be used to expressing themselves verbally, and whether you choose to do it in the form of written work, as a game, in a circle or by reading relevant books, it will all go towards creating a bond within the class and a certain level of harmony. Encourage discussion and friendship.

Above all, celebrate their unique characteristics. Point out their differences and make it clear that it is acceptable, within the bounds of your classroom and the school, to be themselves, and be proud of it. Many children may have come from difficult backgrounds and be unaccustomed to being unconditionally accepted. You may experience some resistance in the early days, as many of them will have shouldered labels that are tough to shift. But believe in them; show them that you have faith in their ability to shine in one way or another. You'll soon have them in the palm of your hand.

Creating an Outlet

This may seem a common-sense technique, but it is one often overlooked by parents. Our expectations (*see page 29*) are often simply too high, and all children need time and an outlet to:

- be themselves
- explore their environment
- make decisions

- work through problems
- burn off a little energy and steam

Today's children are expected to conform from a much earlier age. They attend school earlier, their lives are packed with activities and there is much less time for play and relaxation. Not surprisingly, this can cause an enormous amount of stress in a child and it can be reflected in his overall health, wellbeing and behaviour.

We offer little opportunity for children to be children. They are expected to conform to an ideal – not making a fuss, not interrupting, concentrating at school, on the sports fields, on their homework, eating their dinner and getting dressed without a murmur, bathing quietly, and going to bed, where they are expected to fall asleep immediately and sleep through the night.

Where is the outlet? At what point are children offered the opportunity to express emotion, to unload tension, to let off a little steam, to be children, with a natural buoyant energy and spirit?

I've heard countless parents complaining that their children are so good at school, but a complete nightmare in the home environment. If this picture seems familiar, take heart. Your child has learned appropriate behaviour for the school environment and has probably worked very hard at concentrating and keeping his emotions and enthusiasm in check for an entire school day. In the comfort of his own home, he is able to let down his defences and let out all the energy that has been bubbling inside during the day. This is the way it should be! A child's home is his castle – the place where he can be himself without undue expectations, judgment or punishment.

That's not to say that naughty or rebellious behaviour at home is always appropriate, but you must allow some leeway. If your child comes home in a state every day, he needs an outlet and it is up to you to provide it. An outlet is anything that lets the energy flow. Here are some examples:

- organize some fun exercise
- throw him out in the garden to run and explore
- laugh
- tell jokes
- wrestle
- play
- relax

Don't expect the rigid routine of school to be followed by an equally rigid routine at home. Certainly, a routine will help your child to feel secure, but time has to be allowed and, indeed, encouraged, for fun, high spirits, laughter, shouting, cheering, crying or just lying about. If your child is exhibiting signs of stress or poor behaviour, he does not have an appropriate outlet and you will need to create one.

The same goes for a pre-school child. If he sat through your efforts to get the house in shape, waited while you made telephone calls, has been in and out of the car and the shopping trolley and behaved angelically at a lunch with friends, you cannot expect him to be relaxed, happy and calm. He will also need an outlet – time for himself, to express himself, to let his natural energy flow. Just as adults need time for themselves, children need space and freedom to be themselves. Never expect adult behaviour and self-control from a child. If they can learn appropriate behaviour in certain situations, you've done a good job. The rest of the time, you need to gauge your expectations accordingly.

Furthermore, don't be too harsh about their choice of entertainment. If they choose to lie on the floor reading a comic for an hour, don't be tempted to rush them into something challenging, educational or fulfilling. Every child will have an 'ideal' relaxing activity. Find out what your child needs to relax and do your best to provide it. Sometimes all a child needs is some unscheduled time. Give it to him, and see what happens.

Decision-making

This technique follows on from the idea of offering choices. Ultimately, we all expect our children to learn to make the right decisions, but we do need to empower them and give them the space to practise. Sometimes they'll get it right, sometimes they'll get it wrong, but experimentation and learning from mistakes is part of developing as a human being. Too often, discipline today involves setting down a series of rules and expecting them to be followed without a murmur. This is not only unrealistic, but it also teaches our children nothing. When they get out into the big bad world on their own, they will have had no experience of choosing the right path, and chances are they will get it wrong at more crucial stages, and likely with more serious results.

Like adults, children need to have some control over their environment to feel secure, to learn to make decisions and choices, and to have the self-respect and self-esteem necessary to cope with the modern world. Childhood is a time of fun and experimentation, but it is also a 'training ground' for adulthood. If children are never given an opportunity to make their own decisions, develop negotiating skills, plan their time and activities, experience success and failure through experimentation, and feel that they have some control over their environment, they will never have the skills necessary to deal with life.

Dominating parents may be able to mould their child into the ideal person, complete with academic, sports, musical, dramatic and other talents and successes, but that child will be ill-prepared to cope with the outside world when he leaves home. Children who are given no power, and stifled by over-dominant parenting, are much more likely to rebel once they've left the nest. They are also less likely to cope with independence when they finally get it. Over-controlled children have little sense of self and even less sense of the world in which we live.

We need to trust our children to make decisions, and it is our responsibility to give them the foundation upon which they can be made. All children need freedom. There is no question that a child kept indoors in a completely child-proof house will have less chance of being injured, but one day that child will need to go out into the world and he will have no experience of correct behaviour or have the strategies to keep him safe. Giving a child some freedom, at an appropriate age, teaches them decision-making and brings experience. It also encourages self-esteem and confidence. They will undoubtedly make some dubious decisions at times, but they will learn from their mistakes. Wrapping a child in cotton wool stifles them, and puts them at risk in the future.

Encouraging Decision-making

How do you encourage decision-making? By offering some appropriate freedom. Parenting involves teaching children to behave maturely in every situation. Giving an immature child freedom for which he is not ready will not encourage growth. He'll probably feel frightened, out of control or confused – overwhelmed by decisions that he is not yet equipped to make. The point is to assess your child's individual capabilities and to offer freedoms appropriate to that. It doesn't mean sending a child out unarmed into the world. It means providing, as your child grows, the tools for dealing with situations and experiences and then giving him some space to experiment.

Give him a little of his own money and encourage him to choose what he does with it. Money teaches responsibility and offers a little freedom in which to make decisions. Too much money can encourage materialism, but as money is a part of our world, like it or not, he will need to get used to dealing with it and it can offer him a little personal power.

Give responsibility. Get a fish, a hamster or another pet and make it your child's own responsibility. Buy a plant, or give your child a section of the garden to call his own. Leave him in charge of a younger sibling for 10 minutes while you make a telephone call. Responsibility encourages children to use their own resources in order to cope. If you smother your child and withdraw his responsibility, reducing his time for freedom to suit your own schedule, he will never learn to rely upon himself, to take pleasure in his own achievements, to feel the glow of completing or looking after something successfully. He will never learn to make his own decisions, and that will impact upon his behaviour both now and in the future.

Older children and adolescents need to be given the freedom to grow and to learn through their experiences. It can be difficult for many parents to let go, perhaps viewing the end of control over their child's life, but it's an essential part of growing up. Gauge the correct age for different independent activities by talking to their friends' parents, and working out what is appropriate for your individual child. Set down rules about regular phone calls home, particularly if your child is late, suitable activities and guidelines. Try to keep the channels of communication open so that your child feels confident confiding in you. You'll feel more comfortable if you have a vague idea of what is going on in his life. But once you've established the ground rules, sit back and give some freedom and responsibility. Your child will inevitably make mistakes, do silly things and push the rules to the limit, but these are part of the learning curve and necessary steps to adulthood. They make decisions and they learn the consequences.

Ultimately, we need to trust in our children to make the correct decisions, and having given them love, support and moral values, we do need to allow them the scope to face the outside world armed with self-respect and self-belief.

Emotional Vocabulary

Children need to be taught to express themselves, and they need to learn the vocabulary to do so. Boys, in particular, have been much neglected on the emotional interaction front. In fact, if you ask the majority of boys 'How do you feel about that?', you are likely to get nowhere. They might talk about how they approached a problem, or divulge a plan for setting something right, but most boys do not easily express emotion, largely because boys are characteristically different from girls in their emotional output. Those differences are enhanced by a culture that supports emotional development for girls and discourages it in boys.

As they get older, most children are discouraged from outward displays of emotion, and they learn that it is better to hide feelings than to incur the teasing or wrath of a tired parent, a sibling or a peer. Without emotional literacy, children are left to manage conflict, adversity and change in their lives with a limited emotional repertoire. They are, effectively, faced with inexplicable, confusing and even frightening situations and changes that they do not have the tools to address or express.

In terms of discipline, this can have serious implications. Children who are frustrated, frightened, under pressure and unable to express themselves will need to find an outlet. This often manifests itself in the form of:

- tantrums
- anger
- belligerence
- tearfulness
- whining
- even rebellious behaviour

Regular communication is one of the keys to successful interaction and discipline within the family unit, and it is something children carry with them for the rest of their lives. If they are able to get their points across, verbalize how they are feeling and what they want or expect and make themselves understood, they have the tools they need to understand *themselves*.

They also develop the capacity to understand the way others are feeling. This creates empathy for others and, not surprisingly, respect. They also learn how to analyse why they are feeling they way they are, and often sort out their own behaviour long before you need to.

Help your child by giving him the words:

- 'You must be feeling very disappointed'
- 'That must have made you very sad'
- 'I can see that you are excited'
- 'You must feel proud of yourself'
- 'You should be thrilled'
- 'It's no wonder you are feeling angry'

Give him the words and teach him how they are used.

If your child is reluctant to express himself, encourage him. For example, 'You must be feeling very cross about being overlooked for the football squad ...' and then let him expand upon this. 'You must be feeling very sad that you weren't invited to X's birthday party ...', 'If I were you, I would be very proud of myself ...' Use the words he needs to learn: proud, happy, excited, angry, frustrated, confused, distressed, sad, lonely, jealous. Let him know that it's OK to feel even negative emotions, as long as they are expressed rather than used in aggression, or withheld, which can be as damaging.

Explain how you are feeling: 'It hurts me when you continually shout and call me names'; 'I feel sad when we argue all the time'; 'It really lifts my spirits to be able to talk to you like this'; 'I am frustrated that you aren't willing to consider my point of view.' If a child learns that it is acceptable to feel, he won't be ashamed to admit it.

Much aggression is caused by an inability to express feelings. When we suppress emotions, they have a tendency to boil over from time to time. In children in particular, they can come out as violence and loss of physical control. Most aggression and attention-seeking behaviour can be curtailed by regular expression and exchange of feelings.

Expectations

There are three elements to the subject of expectations: analysing your expectations, making them clear to your children, and then taking their expectations into consideration.

Analysing Your Expectations

First and foremost, many parents are guilty of having inflated expectations of their children. Think back to your own childhood – it's likely that you had a lot more freedom than the children of today. For various reasons, children now have little time to call their own, with highly orchestrated schedules of activities, homework and school. There are very few hours when children are left to their own devices, to explore their environments, to play within an undemanding set-up, to get outdoors and let off some steam without the overly watchful eye of a parent, to have the space to create games, think things through, rest and relax.

Today's parents seem to have little tolerance for boredom or 'laziness', both of which are fundamental to emotional health. The reason for this is partly societal, in that everyone is expected to be the best and to fill their time with mind- or talent-expanding activities. It also has to do with unhappy parents living their lives through their children, making up for lost opportunities and trying to give their children the best possible start in life.

The offshoot of this sort of parenting is that children are under enormous pressure, and this often equates to poor behaviour. All of us take some time for ourselves – watching television, having a drink and a chat, relaxing with a book or the newspaper or going to the gym for a

sauna and some exercise. Despite this, we seem unable to tolerate the fact that our children also need time for relaxation (*see 'Creating an Outlet', page 21*). We expect them to behave beautifully at all times, while working towards achieving the status of 'superkid'.

Take a look at your expectations. If your child is frustrated, whiny, rebellious and even angry a lot of the time, look at what's expected of her. Chances are she doesn't have enough time to call her own. Consider, too, what type of behaviour you expect from her, and work out if it is actually realistic. Remember that children go through a whole range of experiences on the path to adulthood. In the process, they learn to deal with emotions, understand their own feelings and those of others and develop the art of self-control. Let them run off some steam from time to time. Let them show how they are feeling. If you expect too much from your children, they will feel like failures because it will seem to them that it is impossible to win your approval.

A NSPCC poll in 2001 showed that parental approval was highly regarded by 78 per cent of children surveyed. The vast majority of our children are, then, performing with a view to achieving recognition from their parents. You will make it much easier for them – and far less stressful – if you can be clear about what you want and ensure that your expectations are realistic.

Make Your Expectations Clear

The second element is to set your expectations, clearly and concisely. This can be done in the context of a family meeting or on a one-to-one basis. It's a technique that works as beautifully in the classroom as it does at home, in the grocery store or on the football pitch. At the outset of every day, term, week, match or whatever, make it clear to all involved what is expected. You cannot count on children to read your mind.

When I coach my football team, I tell them at the outset of every new season, and then again during training sessions, what type of behaviour I expect and what I want to see from them. They know where they stand, and if they move outside those boundaries, they also know that there will be a penalty to pay. Use it at the grocery store with small children: 'I expect to be able to go through the shop with you. I would like you to stay with me and not take anything off the shelves, or run off. The treats I'd like to buy today are XXX, but we won't be buying anything else. If you can help me get this done quickly, we will get a XXX (chocolate bar, magazine, trip to the park) on the way home.' Sounds simple? It is. All children need to know what is expected of them.

Find Out What Your Children Expect

The final element involves analysing their expectations. A great deal of poor conduct is due to frustration, anger or a sense of being misjudged or mistreated. At the start of any outing or planned event, or even just at the beginning of the week, work out what your child expects from the situation. If they are looking forward to a shopping trip because they are secretly hoping you are going to allow them to buy that new Playstation game, you need to know that in advance. It may be that this isn't in your plans and making that clear at the outset will help to prevent any feelings of disappointment which could lead to trouble. You need to develop strong channels of communication and keep them open at all times so that your children can entrust you with their expectations without fear of recrimination. If they sometimes get what they perceive to be important – and remember, perception is everything, and it differs between all children – they will feel satisfied. If everyone's expectations are clear, a middle ground can be negotiated and everyone comes away feeling happier.

Explanations

Discipline is the art of teaching respect. If you do not take on board the 'teaching' element of the equation, you will never get across the reasons why certain behaviours are acceptable and others are not. Take the time to explain why you want things done a certain way, or why it is not a good idea to do things another way. There's no point in shouting at a child who has fed his breakfast toast into the video machine. No one ever told him not to do it; it probably seemed like a good idea at the time; and how is he to know that you will be landed with an expensive bill to retrieve it?

At every opportunity, take time to explain what you expect, what others expect and why. It's no good citing rules or 'it's the law' to children because it doesn't give them any real insight into why a behaviour should not be repeated. You need to make it crystal clear. Stealing is wrong because it involves taking something that isn't yours, and it hurts the person who has been stolen from. How would you feel if someone took the money you'd been saving? Running through the supermarket at top speed is annoying for other shoppers because they don't have much time and they want to get through as quickly as possible, as we do, so that they can get on with the fun things in their lives. Some of the shoppers are older and don't have patience with younger people. As boring or silly as it sounds, it does help to make clear why things should be done a certain way.

Family Meetings

The best way for all members of a family to set down their expectations is a regular family meeting. This doesn't have to be a formal or time-consuming event, but it does have to take place frequently enough to keep tabs on behaviour, which will be ever-changing. Every family member, from age two upwards, can take part. It simply involves parents pointing out problem areas within the household – perhaps there is too much fighting, or little regard for property, or not enough help with housework. Anything goes. If you see conduct that could be improved, now is the time to bring it up.

Let children have a say, too. Point out why you aren't happy with the way things are working at present, and give them a chance to speak their minds. What would they like to see? When everyone is happy with the changes on the cards, it's time to set down some family rules (*see below*).

Try not to make this an arduous process. Teenagers in particular will be very reluctant to sit down if they know they are going to get a bashing, and they have plenty of other things they'd rather be doing. Fit it in after Sunday lunch, or after homework on a particular night, perhaps once or twice a month. Streamline the process so that it takes only 20 or 30 minutes. You may find that there are very few times when your whole family is together, and making time to sort out the family dynamic shows a willingness to listen and to improve harmony for all involved.

Family Rules (for parents, too!)

Establishing expectations can have a dramatic effect on your children's behaviour. You will need to sit down as a family to decide what is and is not appropriate. Focus on problem areas. For every rule, decide upon the behaviour you would like to see. Here are some examples:

- I won't play my stereo loudly past 10pm. I will respect the fact that other people in the family need to relax and sleep.

- I won't make a fuss about getting dressed in the morning. I will get dressed before I watch cartoons or eat my breakfast.
- I won't fight with my brother. I will treat my brother the way I would like him to treat me.
- I won't come home after 10pm (adolescents). I will call if I am running late and I will always tell my parents where I am going to be.
- I won't have a tantrum if I don't get a treat at the supermarket. I will choose a treat in advance and not ask for anything else.
- I won't argue about doing my homework. I will do my homework after school (after dinner, after 10 minutes on the computer, etc.).
- I won't suck my thumb throughout the day. I will only suck my thumb at bedtime.

For every rule that is satisfactorily maintained, offer a 'reward' (*see page 62*). Obviously, it would be impractical to give a treat for everything done properly, but there are many ways of rewarding children.

Remember that these rules will soon become a way of life, and you can drop them when they do so. Family rules will need to be updated constantly in order to be effective. There is no point in giving stars for getting dressed in the morning if your child has been doing it successfully, of her own volition, for a month. Change the rules, dropping and adding, as your child grows and develops.

For rules that are broken, a penalty (*see page 84*) will need to be determined. Encourage your child to choose his own penalty. You'll find that children are much harder on themselves than you will ever be!

Parents need rules, too! If the whole family is to take part, your children must be allowed to expect certain behaviours from you. Ask them what changes they'd like to see. If you lose your temper easily, one of your rules could be to avoid shouting. If your children think that you spend too much time on the telephone, you could agree to keep telephone calls to a minimum during certain hours. It's all about respect for one another, and you need to show equal determination to please them. Choose your own reward – a week without shouting could mean some time to yourself on a Sunday morning to read the papers in peace, or a long telephone call without constant interruptions. And what about a penalty? This is where it can become good fun! My children suggested that I should not be allowed to have a glass of wine with my dinner if I broke our rules. Another friend's children said that she couldn't listen to the radio when she was relaxing if she broke the rules. Children have a terribly strong sense of justice and they will take things very seriously if you encourage them to do so.

Make it fun! Don't go wild, but choose, say, five or six rules for each member of the family, and talk about them at length. Make sure everyone is happy with the rewards and the penalties, and hold family meetings from time to time to reassess.

Step-parents

Disciplining as a step-parent is an undeniably difficult job. It's particularly hard if you have children yourself, with a clear idea of how you would like to raise them. The most important element of any discipline is consistency. That means you and your new partner must come to some agreement about how the children will be disciplined and how you will approach their upbringing. Whatever you decide – and you must be prepared to make some compromises – it is important that you both stick to it.

There are several potential problems, but none is insurmountable. The first is that the children may well have a different discipline policy with their other parent. Although it can be confusing at first, the children will soon cotton on to your routine, your expectations and your way of doing things. As long as they know where they stand within your environment, they will feel secure. They will also learn to respect your wishes, as long as all discipline is undertaken with love and care. You'll undoubtedly hear shrieks of 'We don't do it that way at home', but gently and regularly point out that things are different here – not that they are wrong at home – simply geared in another direction.

Another problem is undertaking the discipline yourself. There will probably be some resentment, and you may not get a great deal of respect as an authority figure in the early days. But it's important that you stick firmly to your principles. All of the techniques and tools in this book are based around love and respect, and these can be offered, whether they are returned or not. You don't need to go down hard on the children, but you must make it clear that the family rules are here to stay, and so are you. Discipline is not about being a wicked stepparent; it's about guiding children in the right direction for all the right reasons. Even the most stubborn child will eventually respect that.

You are perfectly entitled to have different rules in your house, but the key is to outline your expectations from the outset. Make it clear what you expect, and set those rules in place. You will meet with resistance, some rebellion, aggression, anger and rudeness. These are usually attempts by children to test the boundaries, to see where they stand. Children who have been bereaved or have suffered the break-up of a family will feel insecure and have a host of emotions that they may not know how to deal with. Much of this will manifest itself in bad behaviour. Don't panic or lose your cool. The key word is patience. Understanding goes a long way too. Let them test those boundaries until they feel comfortable. If you shift them, in a moment of exhaustion, frustration or anger, you'll have to start all over again.

Get support wherever you can. The early days are bound to be tricky. But with a genuine wish to put things on an even keel, you will eventually succeed in creating a harmonious household.

Family Time

Time together as a family is at a premium these days but it is crucial for maintaining family harmony and understanding the way other family members think and operate. It also offers an opportunity for children and parents to express themselves in the context of a secure environment. Most importantly, perhaps, it develops bonds that will remain with your children for life. Family is important. Make sure they learn, from an early age, to make time for it.

The primary function of the family is the optimum development of each member. The meeting of the reasonable and basic needs of each family member is the cornerstone of individual fulfilment. This responsibility needs to be shared and, as children grow older, they need to be encouraged to take on more responsibility for meeting their own needs. The way that parents meet their own and their children's needs forms the model that children will adopt later on in meeting these needs themselves.

Lack of family time within the home is sometimes an issue that needs to be tackled within a problematic family. The more family members interact with one another, the greater the cohesiveness and the closeness within the family. It was once a catch-cry that 'the family who prays together stays together'. But it takes more than one type of interaction to create bonds between family members. The following examples illustrate what is needed:

- listening
- helping
- sharing
- playing
- games

- humour
- interest in each other
- problem-solving
- planning
- outings
- parties and fun

The essential ingredient in any happy family is love: unconditional love. Erich Fromm once wrote that 'unconditional love corresponds to one of the deepest longings, not only of the child, but of every human being'. In today's chaotic world, where time is at a premium, this foundation stone of unconditional love can ensure a happy family relationship, and one that all family members benefit from and grow within.

In my book, *Kids Under Pressure*, I developed a quiz for parents to analyse how happy their families really are. I have reprinted it here, simply for the purpose of drawing to your attention the elements of a happy family. There are no points for right answers, but if the majority of your answers are 'no', you may want to look at ways to make some changes. And spending time together as a family is one of the best ways you can do that.

How Healthy is Your Family?

- Does everyone in the family have an equal voice and recognition?
- Do you feel that your family members respect one another and you?
- Do all family members take pride in the others' achievements?
- Do you have a family system for recognizing achievement?
- Do you eat together as a family at least three times a week?
- Do you share family activities at least three times a week?
- Does every family member have time to be alone?
- Does every family member have separate interests, activities and hobbies, with time allowed to undertake them?

- Does your family watch less than three hours of television a week?
- Does everyone in the family have responsibilities?
- Is your family environment calm and loving?
- Do all family members cope well with stress?
- Does your family laugh a lot?
- Does your child feel comfortable bringing friends home to play or visit?
- Do leisure activities play an important role in family life?
- Does your family have extended family members in close, regular contact?
- Is everyone in good physical health?

Even if you can only find 30 minutes to be together in the average day, ensure that you make it a priority. Nothing formal needs to be arranged, but everyone in the family must realize that this time together is sacred. Read, talk, joke around, tell stories, play a board game, go for a walk, go to the beach – anything, as long as you are together. Given that so few families eat together these days, it is important to carve out other periods when communication can be brought to the forefront and encouraged, a time when children know they have their parents' undivided attention, and when they can let their hair down and be themselves. It's also a time when parents and children can work on establishing and maintaining good relations. It's easy, during these periods, to pick up problems with the family dynamic, such as sibling rivalry.

Good Behaviour Focus

This may sound trite and even ridiculous as a disciplinary technique, but it works beyond all expectations. One of the biggest scepticisms held by the parents who took part in the BBC1 documentary 'A Good Smack?' involved praising behaviour that should be undertaken anyhow. But the results were staggering, and all of the children involved positively blossomed when the good things they did were recognized and noticed.

The problem is that most parents are so busy and tired that the only time a child's behaviour gets any real interest or attention is when it is unacceptable or disruptive. And a child's mind soon equates attention with behaving badly. So why not change the focus? Instead of noticing everything that your child does outside the rule book, why not focus on what she does right?

In other words, notice that she remembered to take off her shoes when she entered the house, or to put her clothes in the laundry basket. Praise her for brushing her teeth for the full three minutes or eating everything on her plate. Show that you noticed she didn't rise to her little brother's bait and slug him. Show pride that she dressed herself, came home on time, did her homework without a fuss, turned off the TV when requested and got herself to bed when asked.

Of course these behaviours are expected, but what's the point in doing a job well if no one notices? It's rather like being in a job where your boss picks on every single thing you do wrong and fails to praise any of the outstanding work you've achieved. Chances are you'd probably leave the job and look for something a little more rewarding. The same principle applies to children. If they are rewarded for good behaviour, and their efforts are noticed, they will repeat that behaviour. Over and over again. Ultimately, children want to be loved and accepted, with plenty of positive attention. If you offer these things and show respect for their efforts, they are much more likely to respond with the type of behaviour you want and expect. It's something called 'learned behaviour'.

It takes an effort to adopt this policy, and your child will probably be surprised and then pleased by the attention. It's also easy to forget to comment on the little things she gets right, but persevere. If she feels she is doing well, she'll continue. We all need to feel satisfied that our efforts are recognized.

Ignoring the Bad

This idea follows on from focusing on good behaviour and is an important tool in dealing with children who continually seek attention or behave poorly. Ignoring bad behaviour doesn't mean allowing your child to get away with murder; it simply means turning a blind eye to antics designed to wind you up or make a statement.

This may appear to contradict sound disciplinary techniques, by allowing unacceptable behaviour to continue. But most of the time, children are attempting to get attention in the only way they know is guaranteed to ensure your response. By failing to rise to the bait, you are showing them that you will not tolerate their actions. Even the most stalwart child will eventually give up (although don't expect him to do so immediately). For this technique to be effective, it's important that you stick to your guns and continue to pretend you haven't noticed, or are not remotely interested in, what he's doing. Give in once and you'll find that your child has everlasting reserves of resilience to continue in the future, once the seed has been planted in his mind that you once gave in and will do so again.

By all means talk to your child normally – suggesting, perhaps, that he is tired and needs a break. But keep your voice level and don't appear to take on board that there is anything wrong. Focus instead on positive issues, such as a neatly made bed that morning, an act of kindness to a

sibling, or just chatter about your daily events. You may provide your child with words to express his emotions: 'You must be very upset, why don't you go and take a break in your room?', or 'I can see that you are very angry.' But do not acknowledge anything further than that. Instead, pay attention to good behaviour and your child will soon see that the only way to win your attention is through positive interaction and playing by the rules.

You may find that other people disapprove of this approach and feel that you are ignoring key opportunities to discipline. In particular, leaving children in the throes of a tantrum can inspire many comments and doubts about your ability as a parent. But, ultimately, children need to learn that behaving badly gets them nowhere and that the best times are those they can share harmoniously with a parent.

Older Children

This technique works as well for older children and teenagers as it does for toddlers. Door-slamming, name-calling and storming around the house should all be ignored. If you feel your child has gone beyond acceptable boundaries, offer him a choice with the threat of a pre-arranged penalty. But until that point, let him burn off his steam. If your child tries to shock you by swearing or using aggression, calmly point out that it is not acceptable behaviour, and focus all your attention elsewhere. In other words, ignore him. If he doesn't get the expected response, he'll try something else. Used in conjunction with plenty of praise, this is a very useful technique. However, it is crucial that you offer plenty of attention for the good things – hugs, stars, rewards, praise, for example. If the only time you focus your attention on him is to address negative behaviour, he'll be bound to do anything he can to hold your attention, even if it causes you both distress. Unacceptable behaviour should be met with little interest, or in the extreme, pre-arranged penalties. He'll eventually see that civil conversation and negotiation are the only methods by which you are prepared to communicate.

Importance of Routine

Routines help children to feel secure because they know what to expect. And rather than binding you to a series of inflexible schedules, as you might think, routines allow you to plan and to create space for the things that matter in your life.

Many parents put a sound routine into place when their children are babies or toddlers. Activities and meals take place at certain times, a bath, a bedtime story, a goodnight kiss and then off to sleep. Parents normally breathe a sigh of relief at this point – a little time to themselves is at hand, and their children are happily sleeping in their beds. Somewhere along the line, this type of routine is lost in the shuffle of daily life. Meals run late, are often eaten in front of the television, bedtimes slip, there is no time for talking or relaxing and everyone ends up feeling frustrated and cheated.

The best thing you can do to achieve a certain level of family harmony is to reintroduce the concept of a routine to your daily life. Every family is different, so it would be pointless for me to try to work out your day for you. But try breaking the day into chunks, and ensure that the same things happen – wherever possible – at the same time each day. Some days are bound to be different – on Tuesdays, for example, you may find you have to have dinner on the run to meet the commitment of various activities. But try to make *all* Tuesdays the same. In this way, your children will know what to expect and will feel more settled and calm.

Baby-sitters

Children are notoriously naughty with baby-sitters and the main reason is because they can be! Most baby-sitters are short-term prospects, and usually a bit of fun. Even the best-behaved children have a good old laugh winding up the sitter and, to be honest, most baby-sitters expect it. There are problems, however, when children refuse to be left with someone else, or when they act up to the extent that you are summoned home to deal with it.

The secret is to impart your discipline techniques to your baby-sitter from the outset. Encourage her to use the same techniques, and familiarize her with your family routine (including bedtime), family rules and expectations. You can expect the kids to try it on while you are away, but if they see that the boundaries haven't shifted to any significant degree, they'll soon stop bothering. Make it clear before you go out what you expect from them, and the penalties that they will incur if they fail to stick to the rules. Give your baby-sitter permission to implement them.

If you are a baby-sitter and find yourself in the throes of a chaotic household with unruly children, take heart. You can go home at the end of the day! You can't impose a discipline plan on a family that doesn't have one; it's simply not your role. What you can do, however, is outline your expectations and how you intend to go about things. You can still offer penalties and rewards for various behaviours, although you may need to check it out first with the parents. It's also worth asking, at the outset, how they deal with problem behaviour, so that you follow to a certain extent the family routine. If there isn't a programme in place, don't hesitate to create your own. You can expect some rebellion at the outset, but the children will eventually see that you mean what you say and things will settle down.

Individual Attention

All children are individuals and require personal attention. Similarly, all children are worthy of a little special treatment, to develop self-liking and to believe that they are valued and loved. It's often difficult to fit in attention for each child during a busy day, but even a few minutes together can make a dramatic difference to the way your child feels about himself. It's also crucial for successful, regular communication, which allows you to keep tabs on problems in your child's life and help him find ways to surmount them.

A great deal of 'naughty' behaviour springs from frustration and an inability to verbalize and/or deal with issues and emotions. Regular time spent together – one on one – allows you to develop a rapport where these problems simply do not need to exist. If you show understanding, unconditional love, acceptance and a willingness to see things from your child's point of view, he will develop the trust he needs in order to confide in you. He'll also learn that problems are surmountable and that the solution is not angry outbursts or going off the rails, but a reasonable discussion and the belief that he is supported in his decisions.

Make time for each of your children – whether it's 10 minutes at bedtime and a couple of hours at the weekend – or at different points in the day, according to their moods and schedules. It's often possible to get one child alone in the car when the others have been dropped off to various activities; make the most of your time and, rather than listening to the radio or chatting generally, try to focus on your child and learn a little more about him. Don't ask leading questions, which are bound to be spurned. Simply show an interest. Tell a story that might spark a conversation about something similar in his own life. Show some healthy respect for his interests, even if they bore you rigid. All children will feel flattered and pleased to be the centre of your attention, even if it is only for a short while.

Give every child a chance to speak at the dinner table, and have a rule about hearing everyone out before interrupting. Encourage communication, whether it is positive or negative. The expression of emotion can be daunting for many children and it is crucial that you give them space in which to do so, and that you offer a non-judgmental, reassuring ear.

Children need to learn to communicate without being afraid of the repercussions. If your child confesses that he's broken a window, eaten his brother's chocolate, ruined your best shirt or even, in the extreme, tried a recreational drug, don't blast him. Honesty is extremely important to successful long-term communication. If your child believes he can tell you the truth without a lecture, an argument or a punishment, he will continue to do so throughout his life. If your child has done something serious, let him know how you feel, but stay calm. If he has broken a rule, ask him how he thinks you should deal with it. Most children will willingly offer a suitable punishment, given the authority to do so. They will feel less chastised if they have had a part in the proceedings, if they have been the instigator of justice. With regular interaction, they will become accustomed to conversing easily with you. Understanding and communication are two of the secrets of successful discipline.

Keeping Promises

One of the pleasures of any activity is anticipation, and no one anticipates better than a child. The best way to guarantee resentment in any child is to break a promise or to renege on a deal. Children have an extraordinarily strong sense of justice and if they feel you have not fulfilled your part of a bargain, or have let them down, you can bet it will simmer away and be recalled regularly. What's more, it undermines trust and leads children to believe they are not worthy of your time, energy, money – or whatever it was you led them to believe was coming.

If you aren't sure you can fulfil an obligation, don't make it. Surprise them instead with treats and last-minute fun. Don't plan a shopping trip, for example, if you have an inkling that other commitments might disrupt your plans. Make it a spontaneous suggestion: 'Who feels like a shopping trip today?'

If you promise something in return for good behaviour or help around the house, for example, you must be prepared to honour that promise, at all cost. Children learn that they can rely upon you to keep your word and that when they fulfil their part of the bargain, they will reap the rewards. If you let them down, there is no guarantee they will feel motivated to act in the same way again. If the rewards aren't crystal clear and available, they have no real encouragement to do what you would like.

Kick-off Conversation

This is the conversation that precedes the first family meeting (*see page 33*), and sets out your expectations. It's an opportunity for all family members to air their views, and to agree to a brand-new start. And that's what it is: time to begin again. The slate is wiped clean.

Be positive about your goals for your family. Tell them how you long for a little peace, happiness and fun. How time spent arguing, nagging and bickering could so easily be turned into hours devoted to relaxation, leisure, laughter and freedom for all. Get excited. Announce the new routine with a flourish and get everyone involved in adding the bits they feel are most important. Point out how this new system will benefit everyone and how achieving family goals will make life a lot easier for all involved.

Chances are that your children aren't going to share your enthusiasm immediately, particularly as it involves them making changes to the way they behave and the way the family unit operates. But don't give up. Everyone relishes a chance to start again, to be perceived as a good guy. Focus on the reward element of the system. Motivate them with the good things that can be achieved with a little hard work. They'll soon see that the system works, and as things become habit and routine, you will all wonder how you ever managed before.

Major and Minor: Keeping Perspective

One of the problems with today's disciplinary methods is that they tend to be heavy-handed. Punishments are meted out without regard for the severity of the crime and, not surprisingly, children feel a great sense of injustice. And in some cases they are right to do so.

We've all heard the phrase 'Don't sweat the small stuff', and nowhere is this more applicable than in the case of raising children. If you nit-pick, nag, cajole, pester and pick up on every little infraction, your child will soon lose interest and probably move on to bigger and badder things. Why not? If they are hanged for stealing a chocolate from the sweet tin, they might as well go the whole hog and stay out all night with their friends.

Little things simply do not need to matter. Minor misdemeanours deserve a mention – but not even in every case. If you are hellbent on picking up every single thing your child does wrong, you'll create a child who has no faith in herself, no self-respect or self-belief and who feels downtrodden. If she can't ever please you, she'll give up trying. And that's a no-win situation for all involved.

Angelic children who can do no wrong simply do not exist, and I'm sure most parents would rather have a child who shows a little initiative, a little creative ability and a little imagination. Find your sense of humour and laugh at the little things, saving your punishments and your attention for the things that matter.

Focus on the 'Top 10' Issues

If might help to make a list of the things that really matter to you – the top 10 issues. Make them your focus; set out your expectations to your children, and ensure they are aware of the penalty for infringements. For things that fall outside this list, take a broader view. A chat and an explanation of the crime committed may be enough to set your child straight. If you slam in with a punishment or penalty straightaway, she may become terrified of taking a step wrong, or go in the other direction and decide that your brand of justice is so unfair, she might as well do what she pleases anyway.

Let the punishment fit the crime and, most importantly, let it fit the child. All children respond differently to various penalties, and some work better than others for individual children. If you have a shy, withdrawn child, sending her to her room may be considered an appalling experience. Similarly, a highly strung, rambunctious child will probably not respond to a quiet word in the corner. Gear your discipline to your individual child. Maybe time-out is appropriate for this type of child. She may long to be part of the action, and even the threat of a few moments alone on the stairs will be enough to calm her down. Similarly, when you come to dealing out penalties (*see page 84*), it's important that they are relevant to each child. There's no point in having a blanket rule of being grounded for a weekend if you have a child who would much rather be on his own, reading on his bed. In this case, you'd be better off disallowing reading after a certain time for a few evenings.

Remember that the criminal justice system has tiers and it's important that you implement them in your own home as well. Be open to discussion and explanation; you never know, there might be a good excuse for the odd breach of rules. When children live with justice, they learn to be fair.

Peers

Children will always rate their peers highly and their status among their peer groups will always be an issue. A recent study showed that most children spent time with their friends either every day or most days (61 per cent) and over two-thirds felt they had extensive friendship networks (68 per cent). This type of peer relationship is healthy and normal.

Peer pressure only really becomes a problem when your child is forced into situations in which he feels uncomfortable. There will always be 'pressure', but that pressure can be stimulating rather than stifling or frightening. The key is self-respect. Your child has to respect and believe in himself, and he has to feel confident in his own skin. He needs the courage to stand up for himself and to challenge his peers when he feels threatened or uncomfortable.

All children should have a hidden reservoir of self-esteem and self-confidence. Reinforce this quality in your children and teach them to be independent. Give them some power in their household, so that they are used to exerting some control over their environment. If they feel pressured, ask them why someone else's beliefs should be more important than their own, and encourage them to challenge or question friends who put them under pressure. Teach them a 'who cares' approach to pressure. In the end, who cares whether you smoke or don't? Why should it bother your friends? Who cares if you aren't exactly like your friends? You are unique and wonderful. Celebrate your child's uniqueness rather than struggling to help him conform. You'll encourage independence of mind and spirit that will help him through all types of pressure in life.

Be available for communication and to talk things through. If your child can express his concerns and get your support at home, he'll feel stronger and more able to cope outside the home environment. It may sound trite, but if you teach your child to believe in himself and his achievements, he will be much more likely to resist external influences and feel comfortable doing so. Point out the importance of true friendship. If he's fallen in with a bunch of people who scorn him, or put him under pressure to conform, it may be time to find new friends.

Ultimately, however, help your child to foster friendships and relationships that are stimulating and non-threatening. If he has a circle of friends around him who support rather than undermine his confidence, he's much less likely to be pressured into doing things he doesn't want to do. Encourage plenty of activities that involve a wide variety of different children. If he has some recourse or respite from one peer group, he'll be able to off-load and escape when necessary.

It's also important to remember that peer pressure can be positive. The peer group is a source of affection, sympathy and understanding from people who are experiencing the very same emotions, situations and outlook. Peers act as guinea pigs, as adolescents and children experiment with different personalities and behaviours in the normal course of development. The peer group helps them to define themselves, and it's a step away from being dependent upon parents. In fact, it's a normal feature of development and parents should not worry unduly about pressure that simply may not exist.

Peer relationships do put pressure on family relationships, for as adolescents begin to explore, experiment, question and define themselves, they often contradict parental expectations and even values. The whole issue of peers is, then, a difficult one for children to manage. It can be a source of great stress as they pull away from an entirely parent-led viewpoint, and the support this offers, into a world of challenges and the unknown, where people don't always accept you.

Tips for Dealing with Your Child's Peers

1   First and foremost, it's essential for all parents to accept the importance of peers in a child's life and not to see them as a threat to family harmony. Eventually, all children grow up, and this is one of the steps on the way to independence.

2   Be understanding and empathetic about problems that develop with peers. It's often difficult to relate to what our children are experiencing, particularly if we don't like the company they are keeping. If we keep the channels of communication open, however, our children can use us as sounding boards, and as a kind of moral linchpin, which gives them a feeling of security. Children also need to know they can go in and out of peer groups, but always have the love and acceptance of their family. This helps to balance times when they fall out with friends, or have arguments or 'break-ups'.

3   Ensure that your child has a strong sense of self and high self-esteem and self-respect. Children are more likely to establish positive peer relationships if they are confident and sure of themselves.

4   Although they still need love and approval from peers, children who feel loved at home and are secure in their family life do not react as strongly to peer pressure. If they don't get that at home, they look for a peer group to give them a sense of acceptance and community. Such a group may lead them into antisocial behaviour. The bottom line is, then, to accept your children's peers, but step in when you think they are undermining your family approach to morals, values, responsibility and respect for others. If you maintain communication, and accept that your children will be influenced by others to some degree, it is much easier to encourage them to behave positively.

Physical Affection

The power of touch is well documented and extremely important to all human beings, both adult and child.

Nurturing touch plays a strong role in infant and child development, and research suggests it continues to be important as a way of communicating love and caring between parents and their older children. Most parents continue to share some level of physical closeness with their daughters during the growing-up years, but this can change dramatically for sons. Most parents of boys (mothers in particular) find that this nurturing physical contact with a son grows more awkward and less frequent by around age eight or nine, but the shift is perhaps most dramatic when he moves into adolescence. Many children naturally withdraw, particularly in front of their friends, and this is something we have to expect and respect. However, it doesn't mean we should give it up altogether. Like many other aspects of parenting, physical closeness remains important throughout a child's life. As they get older, parents are among the few people who can give a child the emotional comfort of physical warmth in a non-sexual context, and children need to experience physical tenderness if they are to be able to be physical themselves as adults.

A child who is not touched will feel:

- ignored
- ashamed
- unworthy of attention
- inferior
- misunderstood
- lost
- alone
- unsure
- unhappy

Touch has a language of its own. It can offer reassurance and love that go beyond words. A pat on the shoulder, a warm embrace, a gentle massage, tousling hair or stroking a much-loved little face can communicate acceptance and affection that tell your child how you feel about him. Don't demand affection when you need it. Watch for signs that they need a little reassurance and make it natural. An attention-seeking child may need a little of just that – quality attention. Sit down together with a book and put your arm around your child. If he's watching television, stroke his feet. If he's struggling with homework, give him a hug. If he cries, don't expect him to be more mature. Get down there and be physical. There is safety in physical affection and all children will benefit.

The Question of Bodies

This brings us to the question of bodies. Children need to feel good about their bodies and themselves, and physical affection can provide reassurance that they are attractive and loveable. No one touches things they find distasteful, and if you fail to touch your child, he will get the message that he is something with which you would rather not be in contact, even if this is on a subconscious level.

What does this have to do with discipline? A lot. Our role as parent is to guide and nurture, to teach life's lessons in a gentle and loving way. If your child feels good about himself, he will have the confidence to make the right decisions and the strength to resist inappropriate outside influences. Children who are disciplined without a loving relationship never have the same bond with their parents, and therefore they lack trust. When they feel unworthy or unloved, they are likely to look for other ways to get the attention they crave and this can manifest itself as 'bad' behaviour, or even latching on to peers as a way of gaining recognition. This not only undermines the message you are giving your child, but it means that a whole facet of your relationship is missing – one which can make a huge difference in your child's overall conduct.

Physical Violence

If physical affection reaps such positive rewards, it's easy to see how physical violence can have a dramatically negative effect on your child, his behaviour and his self-image. First and foremost, no one hits something they like or even love. What, then, does a child feel when he is subjected to smacking or any other form of physical violence? He learns that he is unlikable, unloved and worthy of hitting.

Studies show that parental violence, which includes hitting of any description, has two effects. The first is that a child becomes more aggressive and likely to bully; the second is that children struggle with shame, self-hatred and anger. Many children just shut down emotionally at a young age and stay that way, unable to understand or express their feelings as they move into adult relationships.

Physical punishment is about control and a need to gain compliance. These things have no place in a healthy relationship, either as and with children, or as adults. We need to teach our children to make choices about acceptable behaviour. This needs to be done with love and acceptance, and patience. We do not need to set out to 'control' our children. No one has the right to 'control' anyone. We need to teach by example, by showing, ex-plaining and reasoning, and through love. When we smack our children, we change the relationship dramatically and it becomes a power struggle, which undermines any realistic attempt to put a successful discipline plan into place.

We tend to smack our children because it gets instant results. They stop the offending behaviour and they may be reduced to tears, which changes the dynamic of the situation. But think how you feel when you are the object of violence – rage, perhaps, or fury, anger, fear, distress or fright? Are these the emotions we want to encourage in our children?

Smacking children does nothing to teach them about self-direction. All they learn is that someone bigger than them has the right to overpower them physically – a sort of 'do what I say or else' scenario, which is useless as a method of guidance. And as a result, children learn how to avoid getting smacked, including lying and cheating, but not how to regulate their behaviour. They are less likely to internalize the difference between right and wrong or to develop a conscience. And when we make a child afraid, we stop learning dead in its tracks.

Most parents have lashed out in anger, and felt enormous guilt. If and when these occasions occur, however, it's important to apologize, explain the emotions that drove you to lose control and find ways to avoid this type of behaviour in future. While it doesn't make it acceptable, it does teach your child that you are human and able to make mistakes you regret. What is unacceptable, however, is premeditated smacking, used as a pre-arranged punishment. It shows huge disrespect for your child's body and his emotions, and disrupts the parent–child bond to the extent that no discipline will ever be fully successful, all the way through to adulthood. Ruling by fear might produce short-term results, but your child will never have learned the lessons he needs to become a happy, well-adjusted adult.

Power of Praise

The type of praise I'm talking about here is genuine praise, not praise to raise your child's self-esteem beyond realistic levels. Praise is a wonderful tool. Used correctly, it can make your child feel great and shift the whole emphasis away from the behaviour issue. Everyone feels good when they are praised – adults and children alike. But we also know how it feels when that praise is not truly meant. It's insulting and it means little. What's more, it undermines trust. No one trusts a glib complimenter. Praise has to be earned and it has to be authentic. But that's not to say that it can't be undertaken regularly and with heart-felt meaning.

Everyone is too busy to stop and appreciate, to comment on the little things that make us feel good about ourselves. Think of a typical child's day: she's rushed through breakfast and into clothes, out the door and off to school. She comes home with a new painting and you glance at it and say 'how lovely' and urge her to do her homework or to watch her little brother while you finish the ironing. She might have a music lesson or gymnastics to fit in before dinner, and then there is the ubiquitous battle over what she will and won't eat. Everything is running late so bath time is nothing more than a quick splash, and if there's time for a story before bed, things are looking up. Lights out and most parents breathe a sigh of relief.

Look back at your child's day. How often did you praise her? How did you make her feel good about herself? Probably not much and maybe not at all. If she was overexcited, grumpy or 'difficult', you probably blasted her. She may have been disciplined, but she probably hasn't been praised.

I can't overstate the importance of praise:

- Praise produces that content feeling inside that makes your child think: I am all right.
- She learns to feel good about herself, to appreciate and to see good in the world around her.

- She feels loved and valued, and worthy of your attention.
- She sees that she can do good, and that you will recognize it, and her, for her efforts.
- She learns to like herself and develops confidence.

Fit praise into your day as often as you can. If you only praise good marks, she may become obsessed with schoolwork as a way to please you. If you only praise his efforts on the football pitch, he may drive himself too hard to get your attention. If you never praise her, she will continue to do whatever gets your attention, which probably means 'naughty' behaviour. If, during a day, the only time you give your child your full attention is when she won't eat her dinner, slaps her sister, plays her music too loudly or spends hours on the telephone, you can guarantee these behaviours will be repeated. Negative attention is better than no attention at all, and all children thrive on attention.

Be liberal with your praise. From morning to night, notice and dwell on the good things about your child's behaviour, actions, personality and views:

- Praise him for remembering to put down the seat of the toilet after he's finished, even if he does forget to wash his hands.
- Praise her for eating her cereal, even if the fruit remains untouched.
- Praise him for putting on his shoes without being reminded, even if they are on the wrong feet.
- Praise her for putting her gym bag by the front door, even if she forgets it on the way out.

Praise her artwork, her homework, her mediocre spelling test results, her appearance, her memory, her organizational skills, her sense of humour, her silly jokes, and really mean it. Don't just glance at a proudly displayed piece of artwork, even if it's exactly the same as every picture she's showed you all week. Point out aspects you like, and ask questions. Show interest in her and her world. Be thrilled for her achievements, even if they don't live up to your expectations. If your child gets a report card full of Cs, but her teacher says she's really trying, make a fuss. If your child fails everything but gets a glowing personal report, focus on the fact that she is a nice, popular child. Praise everything *good* about your child and what she does. If she feels good about herself, if she believes you like her, flaws and all, she will develop self-confidence, self-liking and self-respect that will spill over into every part of her life.

Most importantly, however, praise your child for just being herself. Constantly praise her appearance (you are such a pretty girl, your hair looks nice today, you've got such a great smile, you look good in those jeans, what gorgeous eyes ...). Children will define their bodies by how others perceive them. If you make them feel they are attractive, you will improve their confidence and their self-image. Fat children, skinny children, adolescents with acne, babies with chickenpox – everyone needs to feel they are loveable and nice to look at. You won't create a big-headed child by praising appearance; you'll simply ensure your child feels comfortable in her own skin.

Praise doesn't have to take over to the extent that constructive criticism, encouragement, guidance and explanations are abandoned. But it should be the positive that balances the negatives in your relationship with your child. And she's a lot more likely to take on board your criticisms if she knows you like her, that you value her and she feels good about herself.

Power Principle

This is a tricky element in all relationships. Power is something we all need to some extent. Given a little power, however, we can become overly hungry for it, and too much power can make monsters of the nicest people. Parents are in a position of authority, which gives them unquestionable power over their children. But it's extremely important not to abuse or misuse it.

Try not to be too controlling. Avoid power struggles where both you and your children are hellbent on winning because what is the reward – a little satisfaction? It's a short-lived commodity and you'll be back at it again in possibly a few hours' time. This type of lifestyle is distressing and exhausting. Better to offer some choices (*see page 16*), so that your child feels in control as well. Give a little power so that your relationship reaches a more balanced and even footing. Only then can you communicate on level terms, negotiate, understand and respect. Over-control is disrespectful of your child, his views, his opinions and his way of doing things.

This does not mean relinquishing your role as mentor, teacher and carer. You will hold the reins for as long as your child needs you. But you will acquire his respect a great deal more quickly if you show that you consider him an equally important member of the family. And when he feels in control, the lashing out, the revenge, the frustration and anger that drives so much of what we consider to be 'naughty' behaviour, will be a thing of the past.

Rewards

Who works for nothing? Not many adults I know. The same goes for children. We all need to feel recognized and appreciated for a job well done, and we need to be rewarded. Many parents argue that rewarding good behaviour is tantamount to bribery, but that simply isn't the case. Look on it as payment for a job well done, a motivation for your child to alter his behaviour towards something more positive, an incentive to continue and a symbol of the fact that you recognize his efforts and achievement.

Rewards are effectively positive reinforcement. They give your child something to aim for, with the prospect of something good for themselves at the end of the process. Rewards are not necessarily material goods or money. They can be stars, which measure accomplishment, or extra responsibilities, freedom or treats.

Stars or sticky dots of any nature may seem outdated, but for children they offer a visual measure of their attainment, and they almost always work.

Rewards should be used in the following way:

- Use stars or dots to chart behaviour that has been successfully altered. Set up a chart with a list of your expectations (*see 'Family Rules' page 34*) and what you and your child agree should change. For example, 'I will brush my teeth after breakfast. I will get along with my sister. I will do my homework straight after school. I will eat my dinner without a fuss.' For every success story, add a star or dot.
- Set up a pre-arranged reward for a certain number of stars or dots. Five could mean a packet of stickers, an outing to the park or the library, an extra hour of television or some time with friends at the weekend. Get 50 dots or stars and the rewards increase. For example, permission to go to the Saturday night disco, another goldfish for the bowl, some extra pocket money, a visit to the cinema – anything goes.

The point is that children will work towards something that matters to them – in much the same way we do in our jobs. And when there are increased rewards to aim for, they will be more likely to stick with it, and see it to the bitter end.

Stars and dots work best for short-term problems. Change the charts as soon as the new behaviour has become habit, or your child will soon get bored. If they lose interest, put them away for a while and bring them out when the going gets tough. But don't underestimate the power of rewards, even in the short term. You don't need a chart to negotiate with a child or even a teenager. A week of tidy bedrooms can mean an afternoon with friends; the same goes for doing homework, being home on time, and anything else. Give them some incentive to change their behaviour and you have one of the greatest motivational tools there is.

While you are at it, do a chart for yourself. If you can manage, for example, a week without shouting, you might be able to negotiate a few hours for yourself at the weekend to read the papers or do whatever is most relaxing for you. Get the children involved in the process and they'll feel a great sense of fair play.

Grandparents

One of the pleasures of grandparenting is that you are normally one step removed from the hard graft of parenting (including disciplining), and in a position to offer treats and fun for no reason whatsoever. There can be a tendency to over-treat a child in an attempt to ensure they find your company fun and rewarding, but it's worth noting now that this simply isn't necessary. By all means, spoil a child (in my book, you can't spoil a good thing), but if you want to ensure a peaceful and harmonious relationship, it's important that you implement a discipline programme as well.

One of the problems is, of course, that things are done rather differently these days, and the methods used for disciplining children in the past are now often frowned upon. It can be difficult to equate the successful raising of your own children with the tearaways who come to visit every other weekend, and you may well decide that your own methods were better. However, it's worth noting that the strict rules and expectations of past generations were also balanced by a certain amount of freedom and time off, which children today simply do not have. They have heavily scheduled, busy, often stressful lives, and they are encouraged to speak their minds and make their views known. You are, in essence, dealing with a different kettle of fish, and traditional techniques simply may end up causing friction.

Work out the discipline policy in your grandchildren's home. Try to stick to the rules as much as possible, while undertaking the techniques in this book. You may find that there are insufficient rules, in which case you are certainly entitled to set up your own when they are in your household. When you are in theirs, you'll have to put up with the status quo. When they come to your home again, outline your expectations and set up a reward and penalty scheme. Undertake all discipline with love and affection and, if you want to, let the rules slide from time to time, with a nudge and a wink – after all, that's half the fun of being a grandparent. But let them know that you are relaxing the rules and that they will stand – and continue to stand – on other occasions.

Show some respect for the approach adopted by your grandchildren's parents. It may not be the way you'd do things, but they can choose the way to raise their children. It's their right. If you find they are too heavy-handed or too lenient, try employing some of the techniques in this book in their presence. They may well see that there are better, easier ways of dealing with things, and you will be responsible for a conversion! Better still, give them a copy of this book and let them make up their own minds.

Saying 'No'

This message is the crux of this book, and one of the most difficult aspects of discipline. How do you say no and really mean it?

First of all, it's important to realize that children learn, very early on, when you mean no. Sometimes your 'no' may not sound emphatic enough and any normal child will sense a weakening and go for the jugular of the 'Oh pleeease' nature. Sometimes, subject to a good argument or some sound negotiation, you may give in. And that's acceptable.

But when you really mean no, most children can sense it instantly. There is a change of tone, a set to your jaw, a steely look in your eye. Where there's no hope of a mind change, the majority of children will probably offer a half-hearted argument, but know instinctively that you will not change your mind.

That all sounds very simple. The problem is that many parents say no too often. They do not listen to reasonable arguments and come in with a negative before they've even seen the cards on the table. They've made up their mind before they've even really heard the plea. This is not only frustrating for children, but it is unfair. No one – adults and children alike – likes to be presented with a situation in which they have literally no power. If, for example, your bank refused your request for a loan, you would like the opportunity to present your case, to ask them to reconsider. It's human nature to demand justice when we feel a decision has been made without the full facts being taken into account.

The opposite is, of course, parents who cannot say no. They feel they will lose their children's affection or favour, or they simply give in to ensure an easy life. This scenario creates only one thing – a tyrant. If you don't say no, you'll never be able to start, because they simply won't take no as an answer. Children respect parents who set boundaries and they feel secure. No child will ever feel confident when they have unlimited freedom, material goods or responsibility. They need to work within the confines of a healthy discipline system where they feel safe and know where they stand. The alternative is terribly frightening. Failing to say no at the appropriate time amounts to negligent parenting and no one reading this book would accept that label.

How to Say 'No' and Mean It

1   Use 'no' only when you really mean it.
2   And then do not alter your stance.
3   Listen to the argument.
4   Assess your child's case and then make a decision.
5   Make him aware that your decision, based on the facts, is final and not open to negotiation.

This teaches your child many things, the most important of which is presenting a good case in advance, thinking through the reasons why he wants to have or do something. It also makes him assess how important it really is and why it does or may not really matter.

When you say no, you must mean it. That's the bottom line.

The situation differs slightly with younger children, but the message remains the same. Try to avoid constantly using the word no. Try to avoid constant negative messages, such as 'Don't do that', or 'Stop'. Children easily become bored by this litany and soon begin to ignore it. And that's where the rot sets in. If your child learns, early on, to ignore the word no, you'll have a much more difficult time re-establishing your authority later on. Save no for the important issues, such as safety or extremely disruptive behaviour. The rest of the time, use diversion tactics (changing the scene, focusing on another activity, for example), or provide a child-friendly explanation of why you do not consider what he is doing to be right. For example, instead of shouting no when your child feeds his peanut butter sandwich to your new baby, gently remove the offending article and explain that babies will become very ill if they eat peanut butter. Ask your child to help you feed her something more appropriate. Matter solved without having to use the 'n' word.

Do not overuse the word, and stick to your guns when you have made a decision to use it. You may meet with some resistance, but you will eventually get your message across and inspire a little respect at the same time. And that's the core element of discipline: respect. Show some respect for your child's position and arguments. If you don't agree, he'll have to show some respect for yours. Take this stance, and you cannot fail.

Self-respect

The emphasis on self-esteem that has littered self-help books for the past few years has created some unholy monsters. Parents bend over backwards to ensure that their children are praised, rewarded, adored – even worshipped – in order to find the holy grail of self-esteem.

Now self-esteem is undoubtedly important. It involves having a positive self-image and feeling good about ourselves. We want that for our children, but many parents go in completely the opposite direction and give children a false sense of their own worth. They pump them up to the extent that they believe they are all-powerful and from that point on they have their parents over a barrel. They've learned how to express themselves emotionally and they've accepted that they are the best. They have very little time for anything other than praise or that increases their good feelings about themselves.

One of the problems with this is that the 'real' world may not recognize your child's genius and he will be set up for a nasty fall when he reaches adulthood, or even his late teens. The other problem is that discipline becomes more a question of softly, softly, rather than a realistic set of tools on which your child will rely as he makes decisions throughout his life.

The most important quality with which you can imbue your child is self-respect. It differs from self-esteem in several key ways. The first is that respect means a conscious understanding of strong points and limitations. It means accepting themselves as they are, not as some perfect child with expectations to live up to and an unreal sense of their own capabilities and weaknesses. While esteem is awarded, respect must be earned through responsibility, cooperation and achievement. If we avoid the use of self-respect and substitute self-esteem, we have a convenient way of avoiding the effort required to succeed. For example, giving everyone a trophy simply because they participated in a race would increase everyone's self-esteem, but not their self-respect.

And self-respect is the linchpin of successful discipline. When a child learns to respect himself, he also learns the ability to respect others – and other things, such as property, motivation, emotions, responsibility and authority. This is because he has earned his self-image and can respect that. The process that led him there will be etched in his mind, and he will be able to draw upon it in different situations throughout his life, when dealing with others and when acting in society as a whole.

You can't 'give' your child self-respect, but you can ensure he earns it. Here are a few pointers:

- Offer him opportunities to take responsibility.
- Give him unqualified attention and unconditional love (enhancing his belief in himself as a unique individual, worthy of such attention).
- Provide realistic goals and praise their attainment.
- Reward genuine effort and achievement rather than blindly praising things that show no enterprise, initiative or effort.
- Encourage him to feel good about himself and his body.
- Praise the things that make him special.
- Teach him respect for others.

It may all sound rather new-agey, but it is easy once you begin. Set realistic expectations and respect the efforts your child makes to attain them, whether they involve matters of discipline, schoolwork, sports, interaction with family and peers, work, responsibility and just about anything else. It's a time-consuming process, but good parenting takes time. Explain why things matter – why jumping on someone's sofa might be offensive; why rustling sweet wrappers in the cinema is disruptive; why hitting someone makes them feel bad about themselves; how the destruction of someone else's property is insulting and hurtful. Put it in their terms, and help them to feel empathy and understanding for those around them, in all kinds of different situations. If you teach your children respect for others, they will learn to understand the concept and develop a healthy respect for themselves. It is that simple.

Sense of Humour

No one can discipline successfully without a sense of humour, and using it is one of the greatest ways to defuse a difficult situation. Much childish behaviour is, in fact, amusing. Rather than heading straight for the rule book and finding a punishment to fit the alleged crime, try taking a step back in order to see the humour in the situation. There is nothing wrong with laughing from time to time and then pointing out gently that although it is funny, the behaviour should not be repeated for the following reasons.

Laughing and showing a sense of humour play a number of key roles in parenting. First of all, they teach children to laugh at themselves – to see that their behaviour is actually quite silly. Laughing at a child doesn't need to be cruel – and it is certainly inappropriate when your child is distressed or seeking attention – but it can introduce a playful element into your relationship, which helps to take the pressure away from a constant power struggle.

The second reason why showing a sense of humour helps is that children learn not to take confrontation and arguments too seriously. They learn to brush them off and move on, not holding grudges or bottling up rage. They see that difficult situations are finite and can be laughed off and thereby defused.

All of us have had head-on confrontations with children, which appear to go nowhere and are seemingly interminable. Try to see things through the eyes of an observer – you have an angry teenager who refuses to bend. You are standing face to face, glaring at one another and engaged in a shouting match. Try to see the funny side. No one can win this situation, and locking horns can be exhausting for everyone involved. Showing a sense of humour, and an ability to admit temporary defeat by laughing, is often enough to allow the situation to blow over. No one has won, but no one has lost either. Many confrontations are simply about scoring points. If you can walk away, both feeling relieved that it's over, you may well avoid such situations in future – there has been no loss of face and no reason to hang on to the issues.

Children are funny. Enjoy them while they are young, and take pleasure in their antics. It's ridiculous to expect perfect behaviour all the time, so why not allow the little things to slip and have a good laugh in the process.

Showing Respect and Faith

Believing in your child is one of the best ways to get results and to build her self-respect (*see page 68*). Have faith in yourself as a parent, and trust that you are giving your child the tools she needs to take the path towards a happy, successful life. Listen to what she has to say. Give her views respect, even if they differ from your own. Allow her some individuality and celebrate her unique take on life. It may always be different from yours but that doesn't mean it's wrong.

When you embark upon a new discipline programme, it is crucial that you have faith in your child's ability to live up to expectations. In a nutshell, if you expect the worst, you'll get it. Show faith in her decision-making process, even if she gets it wrong from time to time. Show belief in her ability to think for herself and behave appropriately. Once again, it comes down to labels. If you label your child, even mentally, with a negative image, chances are she'll live up to it. Instead, seek out the good things she does, focus on them and help her feel she is worthy. This will give her the confidence to go on making the right decisions.

This doesn't mean taking a blinkered view of your child and her capabilities. If she has an argument with a friend at school, don't automatically assume she's right, but don't jump in and assume she's to blame either. Listen carefully to her side of events, shore up her confidence by pointing out what she has done right, and then explain how others might see things differently and how she could have dealt with the situation in another way.

Showing faith and respect has the amazing ability to create self-fulfilling prophecies. A child who believes in herself, who has your support, understanding and assurance, will always have the feeling that she can do things right, given half a chance. And for that reason alone, she probably will.

Slipping

Nobody's perfect and we all have bad days. No matter how dedicated you are to making changes, it can be hard work, and there will be times when it seems everything is going haywire. During these periods, it's easy to slip back to your 'old' way of doing things – indeed, the previous status quo has a nasty way of entering the proceedings without you even being aware it's happening.

In the short term, it is important to remember your aims. We've learned that shouting, slapping, locking horns and entering into a vitriolic exchange simply don't work. It raises the temperature to the point where no one can get away unscathed, or without losing face. Stick to your guns. You may be tired, frustrated and sick to death of children, but it's important to keep your head. Show the yellow card (*see page 84*) and warn them that the behaviour is unacceptable. Give them a chance to make another choice. If they fail to do so, you are justified in giving them a pre-arranged penalty. Remind them of the rules you have agreed as a family.

Let's look at a typical situation. You come home from work and your two kids are battling:

He's stolen my doll – he's a stupid pig.

Liar, she started it. She ripped up my card.

Did not.

Shut up.

OK, that's enough. We agreed that the best way to get on is to show some respect. I don't see any of that here.

How can I respect him, he's a useless idiot.

She's an airhead.

Right. This is your first warning. If I have to warn you again, there will be no television this evening.

A half-hearted grunt is heard from both children, but the warning has worked. They know that a second warning means trouble, and they know you mean business.

It may be that the argument continues, in which case you follow through with your warning. This only has to be done once or twice over a long period of time to refresh their minds. The status quo will soon be restored.

Long-term slipping is a different proposition. When things start to work well, you may let things go a little: forget the rewards, give up the family meetings, never remember to praise the good stuff and find yourself focusing instead on the problem behaviours. There are many other reasons why things may slip – time constraints may make it difficult to be so hands-on in your approach. You may have a new baby or have to travel for work. There may be visitors, an illness in the family or, in fact, any disruption of the normal daily routine. Kids love routine (*see page 44*) because they know where they stand. Any change can send them skittering in all sorts of different directions, and the end result is that your carefully thought-out policies go out the window. It's back to the yelling, arguing and nagging – exactly the type of family dynamic you want to avoid.

What should you do? First of all, accept that this is normal. No one's perfect and things do slip from time to time. You need, however, to go back to basics. Start at square one, with a family meeting, a reminder of expectations, some new rules, some exciting new rewards and a few new penalties. Make sure everyone understands the ropes, and get it all underway. Remember that everyone loves a fresh start – a chance to put behind you all the bad stuff and start anew. Don't carry any grudges about past behaviour. Everyone is given a clean slate and shown faith in their ability to make change. Take a deep breath and go back to what you know works best.

Stress Relief

Stress is the most common cause of problems within the family and disruptive behaviour inside and outside the home. If you are overly hard on your children within the confines of your home environment, you can bet that they'll let off steam elsewhere. And that can have serious implications. Similarly, if you've had a hard day at work or elsewhere, you'll need to let go somewhere as well. Much of the shouting and snapped tempers that occur at the end of the day are simply down to stress – and all family members are affected.

If your kids are stressed, you'll feel the tension. Don't underestimate the severity of the problem: according to research published in October 2000, children as young as eight describe themselves as 'stressed'. More than 200 interviews conducted by a team from City University in London found unprecedented levels of stress in British people of all ages and 'worryingly high' levels in children. More than a quarter of those questioned by the researchers said they were often or always stressed. Half were 'occasionally stressed'. And if you are under pressure yourself, a tinderbox situation has been created.

The answer is to understand that pressure – both external and emotional – can have a dramatic impact on your family dynamic. Talk to your kids about it. Explain how stress manifests itself (irritability, mood swings, difficulty concentrating, trouble sleeping, headaches, etc.) and point out that everyone within the family is going to need to exercise some patience from time to time. If they understand the reason why they are feeling the way they do, and you, too, recognize that your inability to cope from time to time is down to stress, not your kids or your parenting skills, you'll all be much more able to develop a little resilience.

Tips to Reduce Family Stress

- Ensure that every family member has some 'me' time to do whatever relaxes them.
- Keep the volume down on everything in the house for a few hours; better yet, switch off the television, radio and games console and let a little peace slip into your lives.
- Arrange for regular, non-competitive exercise for everyone in the family, to burn off the adrenaline and give yourselves a break from one another. As important as it is for families to make time to be together, it is equally crucial that you have times apart. If you don't, cabin fever sets in and no one can escape its clutches.
- Make sure everyone is getting enough sleep. In our 24/7 society, it's easy to forget that sleep is important. Even occasional sleeping problems can make daily life feel more stressful or cause you to be less productive. A survey in the US showed that children who get enough sleep report a better ability to concentrate, accomplish required tasks and handle minor irritations. In contrast, those with a higher 'sleep deficit' (regularly getting less than required)

showed impairment of the ability to perform tasks involving memory, learning, logical reasoning and mathematical calculation. They also found relationships at home and with friends more difficult. Given that childhood is a period of intense learning and physical and emotional development, it is crucial that children have the resources available.

- Practise a little time management. You may find that all of you are taking on too much, which puts pressure on other aspects of your life. Balancing work demands, time for taking care of ourselves and time for relationships and family can be a juggling act of immense proportion. In a happy family, every member needs a voice. As a unit you need regularly to determine your priorities and values. Regularly asking yourselves what is important in your life and why this is so is a good exercise in personal development. Then, compare these priorities and values to how you are living your lives. Set realistic goals and know your limits. No one has more than 24 hours each day in which to live, work, love, learn and rest. Trying to squeeze in too many activities and responsibilities usually means cheating someone or something else. Make time for the important things in life. As a family, you can decide together how best to find a balance.

- Try to have a watch-free day every week (or if you can't manage that, when on holiday). Let your child do whatever he wants (within reason!) whenever he wants, and don't push a schedule upon him. Let him play, nap, do his homework, ride his bike, play the piano, bang a ball about, exercise or whatever he wants without demanding that he meet commitments. And you do the same.

Whatever you do, remember that stress takes its toll on the whole family, even if only one or two members are under pressure themselves. If you take time for yourself – a little self-nurturing – you'll feel better able to respond to the demands. And with renewed patience, you can teach your children how to cope with the demands in their own lives.

Single Parents

Without the backup of a partner, discipline can be a daunting prospect and there is often little respite from the day-to-day rigours of child-rearing. But as a single parent myself, I can say, hand on heart, that it is perfectly possible. I believe the secret is communication – expressing your own emotions so the children develop a level of empathy that encourages respect and a genuine desire to help you out.

Routine is particularly important, and it's often the only way you can keep things under control. In our family, the routine is sacred. It involves them helping me, for 20 minutes or so each evening, with housework, or changing beds, sorting clothes, emptying rubbish bins and that sort of thing. Far from finding it boring, the children actually enjoy doing things together, rather than having me off doing it all myself, and they take their responsibilities very seriously.

It's much easier to give in than battle single-handedly, and many single parents choose the easy route simply because there are not enough hours in the day, or enough energy, to implement and maintain a regime. But I can assure you that it is easier to get a routine up and running, one that everyone respects and agrees to adhere to, than it is to struggle haphazardly. Because a single parent needs to be both loving parent and disciplinarian all in one, it is particularly important that you combine the roles. You can't be the good guy and the bad guy at the same time, so discipline must be undertaken with compassion, understanding, patience, love and respect. Discipline doesn't need to involve head-to-head battles; it simply involves setting out expectations, and putting into play a system of rewards and penalties that will encourage the type of behaviour you expect.

Make sure you take time for yourself, even if it is a stolen hour or so during the day. Self-nurturing is not a luxury, and in the case of a single parent, it is extremely important that you find time to put things back. Parenting can often be a thankless job, and if you have no one there pointing out all the good things you do, it can be even harder. Look after yourself and you'll find the whole prospect a lot less daunting. Take advantage of offers of help. Let the children bear some of the responsibilities of the household. This doesn't mean robbing them of their childhood; it simply means that they can be involved in the daily running of the house on a minor level. It takes the pressure off you, means spending some time together and teaches them some responsibility.

Time-outs or Time-ins?

Time-out is a commonly used punishment for a wide variety of offences. There is no doubt that for some children it is an experience that breaks a cycle of frustration and fighting. But time-outs can also be a negative experience for many children. They are sent to their rooms, or to a 'naughty' chair or step, in an attempt to punish them. The idea is, I suppose, that they will reflect upon their crimes and come back new and improved. However, the fact is that children don't normally work that way. Chances are they'll brood, plan a revenge attack, nurture bitter feelings and feel a great sense of injustice. For young children, being sent away from the hubbub of the family can be soul-destroying, and they feel genuine anxiety that they are being left out or missing out on something important.

Time-out can be a positive experience, if the goal is properly explained. If your child has completely lost it and cannot reason or see the reason behind a change of behaviour, it's a good idea to suggest a break. Not a punishment, but a chance to get away from it all. More of the 'why don't you go to your room, get out a book, listen to a story tape, play with your animals, listen to music, do some colouring' variety, which offers an opportunity to calm down. 'When' – and this is important – 'you feel better and are ready to change your behaviour, you may come down.' Having a little fun time in his room does not mean you are letting him get away with whatever crime he has committed. You are giving him the space to assess when *he* feels calm enough to *change his behaviour.*

There is no loss of face here, because he is in the driving seat. He chooses when he comes out, and he makes that choice when he is ready. Even adults need to learn when to call a halt to an unproductive encounter, such as an argument. And a little time alone serves that purpose beautifully. Your child will learn a life lesson through this type of technique. He will learn to monitor his own behaviour, and when things get past the point of no return, he'll learn that taking himself away for a little break will help to cool things down until he feels more able to cope. It's a lesson a lot of parents could do with!

Time-ins

And what about time-ins? Remember that a lot of poor behaviour comes down to a cry for attention. While you don't want to reward bad behaviour, sometimes you need to put yourself in the shoes of that little person standing before you. He needs some attention, and he needs it now. Offer a choice: 'You are obviously very upset and angry with me. I understand that this is the reason why you are lashing out at your brother and throwing the toys. We have two choices here. You can go off to your room and have a break until you feel ready to start again. Or you can apologize to your brother and we can sit down and read a story together. Which do you choose?' What you are offering here is a little olive branch. You recognize his need for attention and you are giving him a graceful way to extract himself from a difficult situation, without undermining the rules in any way.

Tough Love and Unconditional Love

Tough love is ostensibly about being 'tough' in order to show your love. Parents with extremely problematic children use this as an argument for being strict and unmoving in their approach to discipline – all for the good of the child. It's the 'it's for your own good' scenario. In my view, this has no place in a healthy relationship. No one has the right to decide what is 'best' for another person, whether they are a child or not. It undermines any mutual respect, and it negates the fact that everyone is unique, with their own way of doing things and living their lives. We are not talking about drug-addicted children here, of course. In serious cases, heavier-handed methods may be required.

In the average family, however, you are likely to be much more successful with the unconditional love approach: 'I don't like what you did, but I love you.' Unconditional love does not mean that everything your child does is OK, but it does mean that you love her, regardless of her actions, behaviour, achievement or anything else. And that's something at a bit of a premium these days. Because of the pressures of time and the competitive nature of our society, children often feel that they have to perform, succeed, win or be the best to get their parents' love and attention. And because of this, they feel constantly frustrated and undervalued. If there is one thing children should not need to work for, it's your love.

Love is a healthy responsibility. If you know someone loves and trusts you, it's much easier to live up to expectations. First, because you don't want to let down someone who has so much faith in you; second, because you believe you are a good person if you are worthy of so much love. And when children feel good, they behave better. It's as simple as that. You don't need to be the tough guy to get your message across. A little love goes a long, long way.

Unconditional love and acceptance give them the courage and strength to explore, take risks, challenge, attempt and achieve the things they want in life. Do you offer your child emotional support? If so, in what way? Do you accept the good with the bad, the failure with the success? If your approach to parenting focuses too heavily on judging your child, discipline, behaviour, achievement, performance and fulfilling expectations, your child will not have the support she needs to deal with stressful situations. Nor will she have the communication channel she needs to express concerns, learn from failure and, ultimately, know there is someone, somewhere, who will love her no matter what she does.

If a child lives with encouragement and appreciation, she becomes confident. If her main relationships are with people who are patient and undemanding, she will have the security to try new things without a fear of failure. She will not be afraid of failing to live up to expectations, and she will be encouraged to celebrate her own achievements and successfully reach personal goals. This will make her stronger and more resilient to peer pressure, life's ups and downs and all the knocks along the way. If a child feels good about herself, and is supported in that belief, she will meet challenges with vigour and enthusiasm. Most importantly, however, she will be happy. And happy people have little reason to lash out, argue, plan revenge attacks, rebel or seek attention.

Turning up the Volume

Shouting, screaming, crying – it not only raises the decibel level in your home, but it creates a tangible tension that is tough to shift. One of the rules in any family has to be a concerted effort to turn down the volume. Watch the reaction the next time you shout. Backs are stiffened, hackles are raised, and the noise level rises and rises to a crescendo level. There's no going back from that. What's worse is that this type of situation tends to escalate over time, so that the shouting gets louder and that elusive peace is all but gone.

There's no harm in the odd flaming row to let off a little steam. But it must be done in the context of a healthy family environment where everyone is aware that it is simply a release of tension. If you have a screamer in your midst, send her up to her room to shout it out into her pillow. Or when she's finished shouting, release the tension by trying to make her laugh. Better still, teach her different ways to release tension – going for a run around the block or dancing to music in her bedroom – and *then* talking things through in a reasonable fashion.

Work at keeping things quiet and harmonious:

- When the noise level starts to rise, get everyone out of the house, or suggest something to reduce the tension, such as exercise, singing, dancing or just taking a great big breath.
- Count to 10 when you feel yourself losing control. This is the time it takes for a surge of adrenaline to abate. Teach your children the same technique.
- Whatever you do, keep the volume down. No one will ever find any lasting happiness or harmony if they can't hear themselves think.

Warnings and Penalties

We briefly discussed penalties in the rewards section (*see page 63*), and this is an important part of any discipline programme. Some people like to use counting: one is the first warning, two is the second, and three means – you're out. I prefer to use the soccer system of red and yellow cards. Yellow is a warning. Two yellows and you get a red. Red card means being sent off, or in this case, acquiring a pre-arranged penalty.

This system works extremely well for children because it is so visual. I've used it successfully in many situations. Holding up a yellow card is a great way to stop an argument, a tantrum, a whining session or anything else that falls outside the family rules. And it doesn't involve a whole lot of negotiation, emotion or useless words. They know what it means and they know what will come next if their behaviour continues. After a while, you may only need to call out 'yellow' or 'yellow card' for behaviour to shift. It's a little like programming your child.

How do penalties work? It's very simple. At family meetings (*see page 33*), set up some penalties, which will be implemented when the rules are broken. Encourage your child to choose his own penalty. You'll find that children are much harder on themselves than you will ever be! For example:

- losing play time on the computer
- missing out on a trip to the library
- giving up an after-dinner treat

Whatever your child chooses (within reason), let it stand. You can consider time-out, if that's appropriate for your child (*see page 79*), but he will need to agree that it's a suitable punishment. Try to keep the penalty in proportion with the broken rule. There's no point in banning television for a night if your child doesn't eat his dinner, but that might be appropriate if he has beaten up his brother!

This system works for a number of reasons:

1 It gives children the choice. They are warned first, so they have the opportunity to change their behaviour. If they don't, they know what's coming because it has been decided in advance.

2 Because they have set the penalty themselves, they will feel less of a sense of injustice (which tends to go with penalties or punishment of any nature).

3 It teaches them behaviour modification. They have to learn – and fast – how to change their behaviour themselves if they want to avoid a penalty. This is a tool that will stand them in good stead for the rest of their lives.

Part Two

. . . .

Discipline in Action!

Adolescents

Adolescence is a period of great physical and emotional change, which we enter as children and emerge from as adults. The course of adolescence is necessarily bumpy, with many rebellions, cries for independence, experiments and periods of self-definition. For adolescents, self-image and appearance become increasingly (and almost obsessively) important, as do their peer relationships and status. This period is also characterized by great physical development, complete with skin problems, growing pains, weight issues and the onset of puberty, in which hormones often win the battle for self-control. Sexuality becomes an issue, which can be at once confusing and exciting. As their children go through adolescence, parents should expect to witness some:

- irresponsibility
- disturbances in sleep and behaviour
- rebellion
- arguments
- sulking
- agitation
- selfishness

Although some of these may be linked to the stress of growing up, they are normal and not usually causes for concern.

Some children cope brilliantly with the transition from childhood to adulthood and sail through the pressures of adolescence. This may have something to do with genes, conditioning and stress tolerance. Furthermore, children with a strong family background, good relationships, high self-esteem and good self-respect will normally find it easier than others to cope with the rigours of growing up. There is, therefore, a wide variation of behaviour that can be expected from adolescents. What every parent needs to look out for, however, are *sudden* changes in behaviour, personality, temperament, levels of activity and approach to life.

The best thing you can do as a parent is to show patience and understanding. Monitor and increase freedom as your child earns it, and show faith in his ability to use it responsibly. Keep the channels of communication open (although don't panic if they dry up for periods; adolescents can be amazingly brooding and introspective, and you might not get more than a grunt) and show an interest in their lives. Show respect for the changes in their bodies and their minds, and remember not to treat them as children. Your relationship will undoubtedly reach a different footing and you'll need to make allowances for this. Remember that hormones can cause emotional and physical chaos, and some leeway will have to be given to allow for the ups and downs your child will experience.

Allow your child some privacy. A lot of what's going on in his life (girlfriends, for example) may be private. He'll talk if he's ready. Just remain a non-judgmental listener, support his actions, and be prepared to be a sounding board if that's all he needs.

Adolescence marks the period between childhood and adulthood, and you will begin to see glimpses of the man or woman your child will become. This can be an enormously rewarding experience, and as your relationship with your adolescent matures, it can also deepen. You'll see the fruits of your labour realized. You'll have the joys of seeing your child begin his journey out into the world. While there are undoubted frustrations and breakdowns of communication during this period, testing every fibre of your patience, you will have the wonderful experience of seeing your child take with him the lessons you have given him and become independent.

Aggression

Aggression tends to be the result of a child feeling cornered, powerless, bullied or unable to express herself. Children who are regularly smacked also tend to be aggressive because they need to exert their will or their 'power' in some way, and it's also the way they have learned to deal with problems. Frustration is also a common cause of aggression. Children often express physically what they cannot get out any other way. This is one reason why it's important to give our children an emotional vocabulary.

What to Do

1   First of all, look for the root of the problem. Are your discipline techniques more heavy-handed than they should be? Make sure you are giving your child enough choices in her life, so that she feels some sense of power. Make sure she's not the victim of someone else's aggression – at school, perhaps.

2   Make physical violence a taboo in your family – we do not hit the things we love, sort of thing. It's a rule that should be part of any family's agenda because there is no place for aggression and physical violence – against people or property – in any healthy relationship.

3   Deal with it calmly and do not resort to aggression yourself. It's easy to be roused into a fury when faced by a hostile adversary, but it's important to remind yourself that something is causing this problem and you need to find out what.

4   In the throes of the situation, use your warning card (*see page 84*) or count. Keep your voice level and calm. Don't explain why what she is doing is wrong. She'll know that. Aggression often masks feelings of inadequacy and frustration. You'll make her even madder if you tell her what she already knows.

5   Distract. Move her from the scene. Find a way for her to let off some steam physically, even if it's just a run around the block or up and down the stairs. Don't lock horns. Offer choices: 'You can stop breaking your brother's toys right now, go for a little run and then

we'll read a book. You can continue that behaviour and you won't have television this evening with the rest of the family. You choose.'

What Children Learn

Everyone has the ability to be aggressive, and we all need to learn to address those feelings and channel them. Talk to your child after an outburst of aggression and try to get to the root of the problem. Give her the words to help describe what she's feeling. Use an example of when you might have felt aggression yourself and let her know it's normal to feel that way, but not right to use it to hurt others or their property. Your child will eventually learn to understand the motivation for her rage and to express it in other ways.

Maintenance

Once you've got to the root of the problem and helped your child to find other ways to express herself, you should be on a clear run. But highly strung or energetic children may still find it an easy way to let off steam. Be consistent about your approach to this type of behaviour. It is unacceptable and has no place in your family. You may have a few hiccups along the way, but with determination and encouragement your child can learn to understand her feelings, and change her own behaviour.

Anger

Everyone feels anger from time to time, and it is perfectly acceptable to experience this emotion. Angry children tend to feel frustrated, over-controlled, a sense of injustice and powerless. The key is to find out what is driving your child's anger, help him work out the cause and then take steps together to rectify the problem. It may be that your child is frustrated by a situation outside the family – school or friends, for example – or he may even be mad at himself or life in general. There are times in everyone's life when things seem never to work out. Anger is a genuine and acceptable response; what is not acceptable is disruptive behaviour or violence.

What to Do

1 First of all, make it clear to your child that you can see he is angry, and that you know how it feels. Whenever possible, use the words 'I am angry' yourself, so that he will see it's possible to experience the emotion without lashing out or dissolving into tears or tantrums. You need to help your child see that everyone is angry at some point, and that he is not in any way unusual.

2 Don't match angry words with more angry words. Keep your temper. Descending into a slanging match only sets up further power struggles and you'll never teach your child anything, or ascertain the cause of the anger. In many cases, the anger is a direct result of feeling over-disciplined or powerless. If you slam down hard, you'll only exacerbate the problem.

3 Give him a chance to work out what is making him so angry. Say something along the lines of: 'I can see you are angry and it must be very frustrating for you. Is it something I've done or are you experiencing some problems at school?' Wait and listen carefully. You'll probably be blamed at least to some extent because children always feel most secure off-loading to the stable people in their lives, largely because they know they will be loved regardless of their moods.

4 Give your child some guidance for dealing with anger – and model the behaviour yourself. Tell your child that you like to go for a run or simply leave the room

and punch a pillow when you feel intense rage. Show how listening to some soothing music can help, as can talking things through.

5   Set a good example. If you lash out when you are angry, your children will do the same. Instead, explain that you are angry and show that it is possible to get through it by talking, spending some time alone or doing something physical to relieve the tension.

6   Look for perceived injustice or inequality, and try to voice your child's point of view: 'I can see you feel angry that your sister got a new bike and you wish you had one too. Maybe that's something we can think about on your birthday. Or maybe you can help me around the house to make some money towards buying one yourself.' When children think their concerns are valid and recognized, a great deal of anger will be mollified.

7   If your child is angry, try letting him have the last word, or show some physical affection. Children will feel a lot better knowing they are still loved; anger can be terrifying and promote feelings of being out of control. If they feel they have some modicum of control, they will learn to use that to modify their behaviour in the future.

What Children Learn

Like all emotions, anger can be controlled and channelled in appropriate ways. If you give him the tools to express himself, and model similar behaviour yourself, your child will learn to do just that. He will also learn that he has power and control over himself and his life. No one likes to feel powerless, and all children need to know that they can be accepted, loved and valued without having to fight for their needs.

Maintenance

An angry child is a wake-up call to some parents, as it can indicate places where you are over-controlling, over-protective, not communicating or even exercising what is perceived to be biased or unfair behaviour. No one becomes angry without a reason and although the cause may be minor in your view, it should be respected and given credibility. If your child becomes angry regularly, it's time to re-establish routines that help him become more secure. Offer him choices that make him feel he has some control. Open the channels of communication to ensure you understand what he is thinking and why.

Animals and Pets

Not surprisingly, this is a considerable problem in many households. Pets need to be taken care of and children are amazingly good at shirking the responsibility. What's more, pets can often take the brunt of a child's frustration, and animal cruelty (although not fully intended) is often an issue.

In terms of responsibility, you are expecting too much if you count on your child to adopt full care of a pet, whether it is his own or belongs to the family as a whole. If you are lucky, you can count on some erratic care, but chances are she'll forget, be too busy or tired, or simply lose interest. If you are planning to get a pet, it's worth taking into consideration that you will be doing the majority of the caring.

In terms of cruelty, children who consistently 'bother' or hurt the family pet are showing clear signs of expressing their own situation. If you smack your child, it's likely she'll do the same to a pet or a younger sibling. Children treat animals and smaller beings the way they are treated.

They may also be over-demonstrative in their shows of 'love' and affection in an attempt to get such much-needed love or attention in return. You may find, too, that your children are experimenting – simply to see the reaction – by poking, prodding, kicking or pinching the family animal. It's appalling to see, but children need to be taught that this type of experimentation hurts the animals as much as it would hurt them to be treated in this manner.

What to Do

1   In the case of responsibility, involve your child as much as possible in the care of your pet, but don't expect her to take it as seriously as you think she should. Plan pet care into your routine – for example, the cat's bowl should be refilled after they brush their teeth in the morning; the dog should be taken for a walk around the block every day after school; the hamster's cage should be cleaned on Sunday afternoons, following homework.

2   Remember that playing with your pets, giving them affection and taking them out is an equally important part of their care. If the children are keeping up that end of the responsibility, you should praise them and be pleased that it's one less thing you need to do.

3   If your children are overly rough with your animals, remove the animal from the scene and sit down and explain why it is wrong to be cruel to animals. Ask them to recall a time when they may have been hit, punched, kicked or pinched by someone else, and ask them how it felt. Put them in the position of the animal, and reiterate the fact that all creatures – human or animal – need love and affection.

4   Look at the way you treat or discipline your animals. If you are too strict or aggressive, the children may simply be mimicking your behaviour.

5   Look, too, at the way you treat your children. It's
    unlikely that you are poking or kicking your children,
    but you may be overly physical in your treatment, or
    you may lash out when you are angry. These are all
    things that can be rectified with a little hard work.

6   Finally, teach your children respect for animals –
    whether they are responsible for their care or simply
    playing with them. Respect is the backbone of
    discipline. Make it clear that it's acceptable to feel
    angry or frustrated, but that it is not OK to take it out
    on others, including pets.

What Children Learn

Even if she isn't taking on full responsibility for a pet, your
child will learn that animals need care, and lots of it. If
you involve her as much as possible in the proceedings,
she will learn to take pride in her contribution. Ensure you
praise her help as often as possible so that it becomes
positive, learned behaviour.

In the case of pet abuse, children can learn that it is not
right to hurt animals, under any circumstances. They can
learn to treat others respectfully, because you have shown
them that you understand and respect them and their
feelings. They learn to channel their anger or frustration in
other directions.

Maintenance

You may find that the behaviour crops up from time to
time, when your child is at the end of her tether. Simply
reiterate the message. Show your child some respect, and
she will eventually learn to respect other members of the
family, including the pets. Validate her feelings, but teach
her, once again, how to channel them in other directions.
A good run in the park with the dog may be one of the best
ways to do this!

Annoying Habits

Nose-picking, grinding teeth, biting fingernails, clicking their tongues, sucking their thumbs, snuffling, repeating 'cool' phrases repeatedly – there is probably no end to the habits that children pick up. At times they seem designed solely to wind up their parents.

What to Do

1   Most children adopt at least one annoying habit during their childhood. The first thing you need to do is ask yourself why it bothers you. If safety issues are not involved, the very best thing you can do is ignore it. If you continually draw attention to something, they are bound to focus on it too, and that means it's continually in their thoughts. This makes it harder than ever to shift.

2   Remember that almost all annoying habits are outgrown. There are very few women walking down the aisle with a dummy in their mouths or a comfort blanket tucked under their arms. Similarly, most university students are unlikely to be found picking their noses in public.

3   If you continue to draw attention to the behaviour, it is likely to continue for that reason alone. Kids love attention, of any description. And if you offer it on a plate, they are given every reason to continue.

4   Some habits, such as nail-biting, grinding teeth, thumb-sucking and most regressive behaviours, are stress-related, so you will need to look at your child's life and see if he is under undue pressure at school, in the playground or at home.

5   Ask a question: 'Why do you bite your nails?' and wait for the answer. 'Because they taste nice,' is a common response. Don't judge or say it's bad or

wrong. You could point out that nails look much nicer when they are cared for, and show them how to clip and/or polish them. Work on ways to change the behaviour without actually saying it's wrong.

6 In the case of something like thumb-sucking, which could damage teeth and the development of your child's jaw, suggest that it should only happen at night-time. Point out your concerns (without making him feel silly or guilty), and offer to help him put a plan into action to give it up. Reward effort. Star charts are always good for this sort of thing. Offer loads of attention for the times he manages to avoid the behaviour, and ignore it when he continues.

7 Remember that pressure to make a child stop a habit is much worse for him than the habit will ever be. All children need to be loved unconditionally, warts and all. If you make them feel that something as silly as a habit changes the way you view them, or the way you feel about them, you are more than likely to make them feel insecure.

What Children Learn

That they are accepted and loved, despite the fact that they aren't perfect. That habits can be comforting for periods of time, but that they have the power within themselves to change them, when they choose to.

Maintenance

When children are unhappy or stressed, they can develop silly habits as part of the stress reaction. They can also regress to childlike behaviours, such as thumb-sucking. Try to ignore the habits and focus on the cause. Your child will need support, love and help with sorting out the problems in his life, rather than feeling that you are judging him and applying pressure as well.

Apathy

Children all have the propensity to be lazy and to procrastinate. What is more worrying, however, is apathy, which involves your child showing little or no interest in things, and exhibiting no sense of get-up-and-go. She may say that she 'can't be bothered' or that she 'doesn't feel like it', when you encourage her to become involved or to get on with things, but that is unlikely to be the real reason. Children become apathetic when they are under pressure, and feel that they need to close down to some extent as a sort of self-preservation. They also develop apathy when they are afraid of trying something, perhaps because they have not been successful in the past, because they don't think they will live up to your expectations, or they simply do not have the confidence and the self-belief to give it a go.

What to Do

1   First of all, it needs to be made clear that trying something is as good as succeeding. Anyone who has the determination and courage to get out there and give something a go deserves a pat on the back. Ensure your child knows this and realizes that making mistakes, getting things wrong and failing are not criminal offences, but a part of life.

2   Take steps to boost her self-respect, so that she does actually have the belief that she is good enough. Children who don't believe in themselves rarely try anything for fear of failure. If and when they do try, they tend to be so negative about their prospects that they do end up failing.

3   Be positive. Focus on your child's strengths, and set up situations where you know she will succeed. With a few good experiences under her belt, she will know that it's possible to be good enough.

4 Encourage your child to set some achievable goals –
at the beginning of every term, for example. Work out
what matters to her – getting a B in maths, making the
netball team at school, getting a swimming badge,
making some new friends or even mastering a tune on
the guitar. Help her to meet these goals by breaking
them into manageable chunks. Not only is this less
daunting, but she can experience small successes
along the way, and if there are setbacks, they are
small enough to overcome.

5 Show enthusiasm for things yourself. If you are
always negative about new situations or complaining
about problems, she'll never see that life is for living
and enjoying.

6 Serious apathy is a sign of depression (*see page 131*),
and may be cause for some concern.

7 Remember, too, that all children experience periods
when they want to batten down the hatches and
spend a little time nurturing themselves. Don't show
disappointment or disapproval at this type of
behaviour. It shows a healthy respect for their
wellbeing.

8 Encourage positive behaviour. Use star charts for
motivation, and celebrate every step of the way. If
your children think they are worthy of your attention,
they'll develop the belief that they can do things.

9 Work out if your child's activities are actually right
for her. Many parents involve their kids in things
they feel are appropriate, rather than analysing if
they do actually reflect their children's interests.
Let your child become involved in choosing things
she wants to do, rather than what everyone else
is doing.

10 Make sure there is some fun in your child's life, and
plenty of free time and play. If everything in his life

seems boring, difficult or time-consuming, he's going to opt out of it all.

What Children Learn

That it is acceptable for them to choose their own activities and to decide when to do them (within reason). They also see that they have your full support and that you believe in them. Mistakes happen, disappointments occur, but successes are equally possible. They only happen when we try.

Maintenance

Ignore short-lived periods of apathy. It may be just a reaction to pressures in her life. Give her space to sort things out, and show love and support for her decisions. Continue to be positive, however, looking forward, making plans, encouraging goals and new ideas, and working on strategies for overcoming any fears (*see page 148*).

Arguing

See 'Fighting', pages 150–54.

Baby-sitter Problems

Kids normally act up for baby-sitters because they know they can. It's an opportunity to show a little power with someone who is usually not quite an adult, but close enough. Baby-sitters often have little authority because they don't know the routines, and they may be unsure how to deal with rebellious kids. They also tend to want to be liked (to ensure repeat business), so they give in. The end result? Chaos.

What to Do

1 Explain your rules and routines to your baby-sitter before you go out. It may seem like a time-consuming exercise, but it puts her in a position of power because she will know what to expect.

2 Explain any of your child's favourite tricks for getting treats or staying up later, for example. With a little advance information, she'll be able to nip problem behaviours in the bud.

3 Show respect for your baby-sitter and support her fully. Tell her that you will stand by decisions she needs to make in order to keep the peace. Ensure that your children are party to this conversation. For one thing, if they see that you are showing respect, they are more likely to show it themselves. Secondly, if they know that you have discussed and agreed the rules before leaving, they are less likely to try it on.

4 Outline your expectations before you go out. Explain that you are having a night or day out for whatever reason and that you do not want to be disturbed. Put it in their terms – if they were out with their friends for an evening, they wouldn't want you on the telephone for half the night, nor would they want to know that you were unhappy or angry.

5 Allow your baby-sitter to offer penalties and rewards appropriately, and ensure they are maintained. Give her licence to add stars to the chart, or to show the yellow card.

6 Remember that children often complain about the baby-sitter, not because there is anything really wrong with her, but because they'd much rather have you there. Listen to their complaints, but point out your

sitter's good points. If there is a real problem, consider changing sitters.

What Children Learn

They learn that you have your own life and occasionally want to go out and have a little freedom. They will respect this, just as you respect their freedom to do their own thing. They learn that they can have some fun (probably on the sly) while their parents are away, while still sticking to the household rules.

Maintenance

If it is a recurrent problem, look at whether your child is trying to manipulate you by making things difficult for you to go out. Stick to your guns. Get a good sitter, someone prepared to have fun with the children and interact with them, not spend the evening talking to her mates on the telephone. But also lay down the law with your children.

These are your expectations, this is the way you expect them to behave and these are the rewards and penalties. Eventually, your child will get the message that driving the sitter up the wall is not going to stop you from going out, so they might as well sit back and enjoy.

Bedtime Problems

This one isn't a surprise. Apart from the odd angelic child, most children create a bit of a fuss at bedtime at some point or another. There are various reasons for this, ranging from feeling they are missing out on things if they leave the fun and head to bed, to taking advantage of a situation where they are guaranteed to get your attention. A few children may genuinely suffer from nightmares and night terrors or other sleep disturbances, and this should not be discounted. For ways to deal with this, I suggest you read my book, *Commonsense Healthcare for Children*, which outlines literally dozens of ways to help your child through various problems.

What to Do

1   If you don't already have one, put a bedtime routine into action and stick with it. Bedtime routines should always be pleasurable and as unrushed as possible. If your child enjoys the winding-down period, he is less likely to feel he is missing out on the action.

2   Offer choices so that your child feels in control: let him choose his pyjamas, a cup for his water, a story and even bedtime (within an agreed period of time). Offer incentives, such as two stories or a quiet game of cards or a puzzle with a parent, if he comes when you want him to.

3   Show him the clock and put him in charge of remembering when it's time to go up. Given a little

responsibility, children normally rise to the occasion and are scrupulously honest.

4   Set up a star chart and make it part of the bedtime routine. If he goes without a fuss, he gets a star. If he stays in bed, he gets two. You can agree on an appropriate reward for a full chart.

5   Use the choices technique (*see page 16*) to encourage your child to get to bed on time. For example, 'If you come now we'll have time for a long chat and a story, but if you make a fuss there'll be no time for fun and I'll be cross.' Children will respond when they are empowered and you can guess which option they'll choose.

6   Make sure there isn't any real reason why he doesn't want to go to bed. Is he having nightmares? Is he genuinely afraid of something? Try to spend some time talking to your child each night to allay any fears. Promise to come back into the room in five minutes to check on him, and make sure you do. Ensure he feels confident that you will come if he needs you.

7   Practise some advance planning to counter any delaying tactics. The usual ones are another story, another glass of water, a trip to the toilet, another kiss goodnight, a hug ... you name it. If your child knows the routine – he's been to the toilet, chosen his own story or stories and has a drink by his bedside – he'll be less likely to find a reason to get you back. If he's toilet-training, you'll have to agree to toilet trips, but make it clear that you are not falling for a planned escape. If he claims to be hungry, make a small snack a part of the bedtime routine.

8   Make his bedroom a sanctuary, with cosy blankets and a familiar cuddly toy. Tuck him in and make sure he is comfortable and content. Stay with him for a few minutes so he doesn't feel he is being 'sent away'.

9 Wind down well before you want him to go to bed. If he is in the middle of watching a television programme or playing a game with a family member, he's not going to leap at the idea of leaving it all. Make sure that the television is off and that all fun has ceased at least 20 minutes before you want to have him in bed.

10 Make it clear that the rest of the family are not up to wildly fun activities while he goes to bed. Explain that you'll be eating dinner, ironing, helping another child with homework or just reading. If he knows that there isn't anything exciting at hand, he'll feel happier about being on his own, perhaps with a good story tape or a book to read.

11 Above all, be firm and consistent. If you give in once, you'll be setting the stage for recurrent battles. While it's never a good idea to show anger at bedtime, which may cause your child to have a troubled sleep, you can make it clear without losing your temper that you don't find his actions remotely amusing.

12 It's not uncommon for children to go into a wild tantrum at bedtime and scream until they get what they want. In this scenario, ignore it. It can be heart-rending to leave a child crying, and you can enter the room repeatedly to show him you are there and that you care. But if he learns that he can win his way by behaving badly, he'll do it again and again, and you'll have a nightmare scenario on your hands. Comfort your child. Explain firmly that you are not going to give in, and then ignore any inappropriate attempts to wind you up or get his way. If tantrums at bedtime are a regular problem, consider moving your child's bedtime half an hour earlier. It may sound crazy, but he may simply be too tired and wound up to sleep.

13 Praise, praise, praise. When he goes to bed when you ask, make a big fuss and show him how happy and proud you are. When he argues or refuses to go to bed, ignore the behaviour you don't want to encourage. Go through the normal bedtime routine, but don't be tempted to battle or argue, which only provides the attention he might be seeking.

What Children Learn

Children need to learn that night-time is for sleeping, and that sleep is important for all sorts of different reasons. Many children act up late at night simply because they are overtired, and they need to see the connection between feeling out of control and being sleepy. If your child's bedroom and bed are a warm, nurturing place, he'll soon equate it with peace and happiness. And sleep problems should become a thing of the past.

Maintenance

With a strong bedtime routine, you should not have significant problems unless your child is feeling upset for another reason, is overtired or stressed, or simply wants to make use of a time when he has your full attention! Continue to offer choices, bring out the reward chart again, and make sure you impose penalties if the behaviour continues.

Behaviour Problems at School

Children need to feel they can behave badly from time to time, to express things that are building up. Ideally, this should all be done verbally, but as we all know, that doesn't always happen. 'Naughty' behaviour is always best undertaken in the home (*see page 76*), where you can monitor it and offer the appropriate response. However, if your child feels she has to be perfect at home, she's much more likely to behave badly where she can – at school or with her peers. She may feel over-controlled, and attempt to show she has some power by attention-seeking at school. It may also be that she is under-disciplined all round and has not learned appropriate behaviour in various circumstances. Finally, it may be that your child is being treated disrespectfully by a teacher, who either shames her in front of other pupils, or has an unhealthy approach to discipline. Either way, this is a problem that can be addressed, and you may need to enlist the help of her teacher/s.

What to Do

1   Ensure your child has some power in her home environment so she doesn't feel a need to find it elsewhere. Offer plenty of choices and respect her decisions. Give her some responsibility to help her feel good about herself.

2   Keep a healthy discipline routine in place but make sure it isn't too heavy-handed. All children need some freedom to be both themselves *and* children.

3   Ask some questions: see if you can work out what is driving your child's behaviour. Hold up your hands and suggest that she might not have enough freedom at home, but also try to work out if the classroom dynamic is not working for her.

4   Be positive and announce a fresh new start. This always works well for children, who like a clean slate. Work together on finding a solution to the problem.

5   If you find that her teacher is at the root of the behaviour problems, ask for a meeting between all of you. Ensure your child feels comfortable enough to express herself and make clear what *she* sees as the

issues. Although her teacher may disagree, remember that perception is as important as reality. If your child thinks things are working a certain way, for her they are. All parties need to work to redress the problem.

6   Listen to your child and show unconditional love. If she feels she is being heard and understood, it might be enough to change the belief that motivated the behaviour.

7   Make sure your expectations are not too high. If your child feels she is required to be the best, and is unsure whether she can be, she may stop trying, and behave badly to take the pressure off her performance.

What Children Learn

She will learn to speak out about a problem and work together to find a solution. She will also see that you love her unconditionally, and that you are willing to respect her take on things, and take her side when the going gets tough. If you take a child seriously, she learns to respect herself. She also learns that behaviour can be modified to meet appropriate expectations, and that there is a time and a place to let off steam.

Maintenance

This is a problem that can crop up from time to time, particularly if you have a highly strung, sensitive or very energetic child. Keep tabs on what is happening in her world so that you can gauge where there are problems and nip them in the bud before they become serious issues. Continue to respect your child and don't automatically assume that her teacher is right. Give her the opportunity to explain things from her point of view. If things continue to go wrong, you may need to consider changing schools or classes, and you are perfectly within your rights to demand this.

Birthdays and Birthday Parties

No one looks forward to a birthday more than a child. It's his moment, when all attention is focused on him. He can normally choose the agenda and is likely to be showered with gifts. Sounds great in practice, but in reality birthdays can be a difficult day for many children. It all has to do with perception. Expectations build up to such an extent that the reality is often very different from how they imagined their day would be. They may have a firm idea of the gifts they will receive and be disappointed by what is on offer. Their party or celebration may not go according to plan. When expectations are elevated to unrealistic levels and excitement raises adrenaline to fever pitch, chances are many children will experience crashing frustration.

What to Do

1 Work out in advance what your child expects. Guide his expectations towards something realistic, and try to make the day as special as possible, according to what he really wants. This isn't spoiling a child; it's helping him to make his day as close to his ideal as possible, and for one day a year, it's acceptable. We all have ideas of what we'd like to do on our own birthdays and we too would be disappointed if someone else had a 'better' idea. Most of the time children demand very little, and it never hurts to fall in with their demands from time to time.

2 This goes for gifts as well. So many parents choose something different to what a child really wants in the misguided view that it is more educational, less frivolous or what they *think* their child needs. A gift is designed to please and to satisfy a need, however frivolous. Why not let them choose and respect their

choices, provided it falls in with your parenting
philosophy and budget.

3   Remember that your other children may feel left out
if they are not in the limelight. Show respect for their
feelings, but don't allow them to hijack the
proceedings. Everyone gets their day.

4   Give your child choices when planning a birthday
party. Limit them according to your budget and other
considerations – but let him help to plan his special
day.

5   Talk through the party in advance and ensure your
child's expectations are not too high. Remind him
that when kids are filled with sugar and fun, things
can decline into chaos, so make sure he doesn't
expect too much. He may not get the full attention
of his peers, which is what he might be hoping for.
They may not respect his special day in the same way
that you do. If he knows this in advance, the reality
will be easier to bear.

What Children Learn

They learn that they are important family members and
that their wishes can become a reality with a little forward
planning and realistic thinking. All children can benefit
from a boost to their self-confidence and being king for the
day offers just that opportunity.

Biting

This is normally a problem with younger children. I have
to say that it is sometimes understandable. Many children
don't bite out of any sense of malice or meaning to hurt,
but because the opportunity presents itself and they
are overwhelmingly tempted. Remember that children are
extraordinarily oral creatures, particularly when they are

young. Everything goes into their mouth as a form of exploration and experimentation. Seeing an exposed bit of fresh young flesh must seem like an amazing temptation.

You may find, however, that you have a serial biter on your hands. It provokes an instant reaction, gets parents up and running and it's satisfyingly physical. What better way to get attention? It's also a form of expression, particularly in young children who can't find the words or the self-control to exhibit their frustration.

What to Do

1   Don't be tempted to bite back so that they know what it feels like. You'll only provoke the behaviour, as they will see it is acceptable to do this to younger, smaller beings.

2   If your child is too young to understand abstract reasoning, distract her from the object of her teeth. She'll eventually become frustrated by having her game disrupted and give up. You can explain to older children why it is not acceptable to bite – how the other person might feel, how they felt if they have been bitten themselves, and how it makes people angry and frustrated.

3   Teach them that whenever they feel the urge to bite, they must do something else instead. Cup their hand over their mouth, stamp their feet, clap their hands. Make it a game so that they remember. In the end the behaviour will become learned, which is your goal.

4   When you see your child baring her teeth, quickly leap in and remind her that she needs to *talk* and *explain* why she is upset. Even young children need to learn to negotiate with siblings and peers to get what they want.

5   Apologize to the parent of the child who has been bitten, and make sure your child hears you do it. He'll

learn that unacceptable behaviour must be followed by an apology.

What Children Learn

Children learn that it is unacceptable to hurt other people, no matter how satisfying it may seem at the time. They learn that there are verbal ways of getting what they want, even if they are not so immediate.

Boredom

Some boredom is essential for a child to find and explore parts of himself. All children need to be alone and peaceful to think, to be creative, to use imagination, to find a little place of peace to which they can retreat when things get tough. They need peace for self-awareness, contemplation, thinking things through, making decisions, getting to know themselves and feeling comfortable in their own skins.

The problem is that we tend to stimulate and over-schedule our children to such a degree that they expect to be hand-fed entertainment and to have every minute of their days allocated. Left to their own devices, they simply do not know what to do because they lack the skills to fill their own time. There's a good phrase that sums up the problem: only boring children are bored. And to some extent, that's true. If they can't find a spark of imagination to occupy themselves, they are failing to use a great deal of their creativity and their potential.

What to Do

1   Ensure, from the earliest days, that your child is left to his own devices from time to time, with periods alone to play, use his imagination, be creative or simply relax. If your child learns that you are

responsible for his entertainment, you always will be. Very small children will obviously require supervision, but give them the freedom to choose their activities and entertain themselves.

2   Limit the time your child spends with distractions (*see page 250*), such as television, games consoles and computers. They need to learn to come up with activities to entertain themselves.

3   If your child comes to you constantly saying he is bored, you can make a few suggestions, but ensure they involve him organizing the proceedings and not you. If he repeatedly rejects your ideas, say that you have faith in his imagination and problem-solving abilities, and that you are sure he will come up with something fun to do.

What Children Learn

They learn to occupy themselves and to enjoy their own company. This is crucial for self-development and it offers them an opportunity to get to know themselves. They also see that they are capable of taking care of themselves from time to time. This feeds a sense of pride and responsibility. In the end, we are all architects of our own happiness, and it's a lesson that your child cannot learn too early.

Maintenance

Suggest that all of your children come up with a list of 'rainy day' ideas – things that can be done when there is nothing else to do. If they claim to be bored, send them back to the list. There's bound to be something there to capture their attention.

Bullies

There are two issues here – children who are bullies, and children who are bullied. You may find that you occasionally have problems with both. A recent study by Young Voices and Oxford University, based on 7,000 pupils between the ages of 13 and 19, found that 1 in 10 reported severe bullying, including physical violence. Many felt they could not tell anyone what was happening to them as their treatment by other children had sent them into a spiral of depression and misery.

The study found that home life plays a vital part in determining whether a child will be a bully or a victim. 'For both the victims and the bullies, parenting was markedly less positive, colder and more controlling. Bullies were far more likely to see aggression at home,' said Adrienne Katz of Young Voices.

Children were far less likely to be bullied if they lived with both parents. Severely bullied boys reported not having a supportive parent and were highly likely to have an absent or unsupportive father. Of the bullied girls, 79 per cent felt anxious about one parent and were more likely to say they planned to bring up their own children very differently from the way they were being raised. Racism seems to be a factor. A quarter of children from ethnic minorities reported being severely bullied, as opposed to 13 per cent of white pupils.

'There are factors which protect children: being bolder and having high self-esteem and positive, warm parenting is overwhelmingly linked to those who are not being bullied,' said Ms Katz.

Previous research by the National Society for the Prevention of Cruelty to Children (NSPCC) in the UK, showed that more than half of children aged 8 to 15 years sometimes or often worried about being bullied at school and that younger children worried most. This study throws more light on this problem, which is known to cause acute misery to many children. According to the NSPCC, 43 per cent of young people had, at some point in their childhood, experienced bullying, discrimination or being made to feel different by other children. Nearly all (94 per cent) of these experiences took place at school.

Whether your child is a bully or being bullied, there is evidence that self-respect may be at the root. If your child feels in control of her life and her environment, and has a little power to make choices, she will not need to exert it on other children. Similarly, if your child is used to being over-disciplined, she may lack the confidence to stand up for herself or to believe that she is anything other than a victim.

What to Do

1 You may well suspect bullying without having it confirmed. Obvious clues are mysteriously 'lost' belongings, inexplicable bruises, withdrawn behaviour and mystery ailments that prevent your child from going to school. If you are concerned, try to encourage your child to talk about it. Ask about different parts of her day, and about the people she likes and doesn't like. Ask if lunchtime or break is stressful and why. Don't bully her into talking, which will just make matters worse. Just let her know you are there if she wants to share the problem.

2 Talk to your child's school and find out what anti-bullying policies they have in place. Chances are they don't know what's going on, and they can take steps to stop it.

3 It's also important that your child develops her own coping strategies. Suggest some sharp retorts your child could use, or ways of avoiding the perpetrators.

Children who are bullied tend to have lower self-respect than their peers, perhaps unconsciously placing themselves in a 'victim' mode. This might be a short-term problem, caused by stress or a family difficulty, for example, or it may be something that needs addressing in the long term. Work on your child's self-confidence (*see page 68*). If she feels good about herself, she'll be able to face up to bullies and hold her own. Practise what she could say to bullies, and help her to feel comfortable remembering and using these words. For example, 'Stop calling me names now. I don't like it and I'm not going to accept it any more'. There's a veiled threat there that further action could be taken, and even the most robust bully fears punishment from authority. The secret is for your child to look strong and confident, looking the bully in the eye and holding up her head.

4   Don't encourage physical violence, which will turn your own child into a form of bully. Violence is never the answer to any problem. What your child needs to do is learn to stand up for herself with confidence. Teach her that violence just incites further violence and anger, which will make the problem worse. All children need to understand that although hurting another child may release feelings of anger and frustration, it won't make the problem go away (*see 'Violence', page 261*).

5   Make sure your child doesn't feel guilty, which can compound the problem. Many children blame themselves, believing that their own actions or weakness led to the problem. Help them feel they are not in any way at fault, and that they are good, strong, effective people.

6   Explain to your child why some people become bullies. Bullies are normally victims of someone else

in their lives. If your child is aware that there is a cause for the behaviour unrelated to her, she may feel more in control of the situation.

7 Don't become too upset. It won't help your child, and she may become alarmed, oversensitive or concerned that she has made you unhappy. Be calm and supportive. Show her that you are on her side, and that you are prepared to display a little of that all-important family solidarity.

8 Some children need an awful lot of comfort alongside the solutions. Don't be too businesslike or problem-focused. Give them hugs, reassurance, love and empathy. Sympathize and recall any similar experiences you had as a child. Your child will be feeling very vulnerable and may need more love than practical advice.

9 Encourage your child to develop friendships outside school, in sports, music or drama groups or even your church. If she builds up a strong network of friends outside school who share her interests and enjoy her company, she'll feel stronger and more able to cope with bullies the rest of the time. Ensure that your child does have a good circle of friends at school, and encourage this if possible. Children in a group are much less likely to be bullied than children alone.

10 If your child is a bully, you'll need to look at why she feels the need to exercise this type of behaviour. Is she feeling out of control or pressured in some area of her life, thereby taking it out on others? Keep open the lines of communication and help her work out alternative ways of coping. Empower her as much as possible, and ensure she feels loved and respected, even if she has made the wrong choices on this occasion.

What Children Learn

Being bullied is a nasty experience, but it doesn't hurt for a child to see that life is not always rosy and that confrontations with other people can and do occur. This teaches them that they are strong enough to stand up for themselves, and that they can resolve difficulties with a little help and support.

If your child has been a bully, she will learn that nothing is accomplished by picking on others, and that the path to happiness lies in maintaining rewarding relationships. She will learn that she can control her behaviour by expressing her problems verbally before they build up to the point of no return, and that she does have the power to make the right choices.

Maintenance

If your child reverts to being the bully or the victim, take steps to boost self-respect by offering a little more responsibility, power and choices in her life. Continue to show unconditional love, while not accepting problem behaviours. Offer solutions and talk things through so that your child knows she can always rely upon you when the going gets tough. Look for problem areas of her life, and help her work out solutions. Take off the pressure wherever possible.

Childcare Problems

Most childcare problems occur when carer and parent have not agreed on expectations and philosophy of childcare. Children can, understandably, feel confused with the shift in ideology and approach. They may behave in unacceptable ways to test their boundaries and to see where they stand. In many situations, your children will be in the company of other kids, who may set examples that you are not keen to encourage. They may learn inappropriate behaviours, or simply copy them to get a reaction (probably because the children in question appear to get a lot of attention for behaving badly). Finally, that old chestnut – if your child is over-controlled at home, he may take the opportunity to express himself and let off some steam when you are not there.

What to Do

1   Explain clearly to your carer the type of behaviour you expect from your child, and how you normally go about encouraging it. Talk through every potential issue, from table manners and talking back to doing their homework and watching television. Explain your routines and how you manage to keep things up and running. If the rules and routines remain roughly the same, your child will find it much easier to switch between residences and approaches.

2   Remember that if the arrangements don't work out, you can find another carer. In the long run, a change is a lot less damaging than having your children learn lessons that might be hard to undo.

3   Children need to learn that expectations differ between families and people. Throughout their lives, they will find themselves in situations where they need to rely upon their own resources to make the right decisions. Explain that your carer might do things differently, but that you expect the same behaviour as at home.

4   If they begin to pick up habits from other children (*see page 98*), calmly explain why you find it unacceptable. Teach them to be strong enough to resist the temptation to show off. You can do this by showing respect, admiration and love for who they are.

What Children Learn

Children learn that the rules they have at home are 'life' rules, and can be applied and used in every situation. They learn to behave in an appropriate manner not because they *have* to, but because they are constantly rewarded (emotionally and in other ways) for doing so. They learn to take pride in who they are, and stand up for themselves and what they believe in. It's a good taster of life in later years, too, as the pressure of peers will undoubtedly come into play at some point. If your child is accustomed to holding his ground and believing in himself, the less likely he is to be swayed.

Maintenance

If the same problems crop up repeatedly, you may need to consider changing your carer. You are perfectly within your rights to ask for routines, rules and discipline systems to be maintained. Children who are cared for by others may from time to time feel that they do not have enough contact with their parents. Explain the reasons why this is so, and ensure that they perceive the time spent with you to be worthwhile and valuable. Your idea of 'quality' time might not be theirs. Keep open the channels of communication with regular talks and exchanges of ideas. More importantly, show faith in your child's ability to modify his behaviour. It's a great motivator.

Classroom Chaos

This section applies more to teachers than to anyone else, but parents can use these tips when dealing with large groups of children, such as at birthday parties.

Chaos ensues when the backbone of a discipline programme is broken, or was not there to begin with. Today's teachers have a challenging role, teaching children from many different backgrounds, all with unique personalities.

What to Do

1 The key is to set out your expectations immediately. It's never too late. Have the equivalent of a kick-off conversation (*see page 49*), and give every child a clean slate from which to start. Be positive and enthusiastic about the new regime, and show the children how it will benefit them (*see 'Rewards', page 62*).

2 Remember to praise and reward children for a job well done. Even if their work doesn't meet your standards, effort, goodwill and kindness should always be noticed and rewarded. Many of the children may have come from backgrounds where they have been labelled throughout their lives as 'bad eggs'. Give them a chance to prove themselves and show faith in their ability to do so.

3 Show great consistency, for all children. Do not give in to attention-seeking behaviour or rise to a challenge by a disruptive child. Like they do in their homes, children constantly test their boundaries within the classroom to see what they can get away with. If they find those boundaries, they will know where they stand. Ensure they are firmly in place. Some children may come from homes where there are no boundaries, but it should help their behaviour to find that they can feel secure in your classroom.

4 When things decline into chaos, as they can do occasionally, such as when it's raining, break the children up into groups. Get them to move around the tables undertaking a variety of different activities for slots of 10 or 15 minutes. You'll keep them active and stimulated.

5   Give them an outlet. A bunch of rowdy children is likely to be in need of a break. A good run around the outside of the school, or even jogging on the spot in the classroom if your facilities are limited, can make a big difference. Children get far too little PE in school these days and it's not surprising that steam builds up to the point where it expels itself.

6   Use the warning system – yellow and red cards (*see page 84*) are great for classroom activity because they are visual and don't require you to raise your voice. If you have made a pre-arranged penalty, stick with it.

7   Never accept belligerent or rude behaviour. Ignore the offender, and if it continues to the point of disruption, remove him from the activity at hand without giving him undue attention. If it continues, go with your penalty. Eventually, even the most disobedient children will learn that they get nowhere with attention-seeking behaviour. Make it a class rule to ignore unruly behaviour among their peers. Reward those who can stick with this philosophy. If they aren't egged on by their classmates, and get no attention from you, the behaviour is much less likely to be repeated.

8   Finally, keep the volume down. If you start shouting, the decibel level of the classroom will rise and that has only one effect: mayhem. Keep your voice level, calm and quiet. Children will soon learn that they have to be quiet enough to hear you.

What Children Learn

They learn that there are times for fun and games, and other times when concentration is necessary. As long as you give them regular breaks and outlets, they will learn to focus. Even the most recalcitrant children can learn to modify their own behaviour, particularly if they know where they stand, see that you respect them for who they are and that you have no preconceived ideas about labels or past misconduct.

Maintenance

For various reasons, all your carefully laid plans can go out the window occasionally, such as near exam time or in periods of bad weather when the children simply can't get out. In these circumstances, start again. All over again. Remind the children of your expectations and the class rules. Set up new charts – and reward them instantly for listening. Redefine the penalties and offer to give every child a fresh start – all past indiscretions forgotten. Change the seating and the routine and give it a go.

Cleaning Rooms

Let's face it: cleaning can be enormously boring, particularly if you are a child with a lot of other things on your agenda. This is one situation that drives most parents crazy and is guaranteed to cause locked horns in even the most harmonious family.

What to Do

1   Break it up into manageable chunks. If your child's room is unbelievably untidy, she'll be daunted by the prospect of doing it all herself. Suggest that clothes are tidied one day, toys another, books another and so on.
2   Help her out the first few times, so that she knows how to tidy efficiently. Suggest a maintenance plan so that it doesn't decline to the point of disaster again. This can be part of the daily routine – at the end of the day, toys are put away, clothes are put in the laundry basket and the general clutter is tidied, perhaps while you run the bath.

3   Ensure that you reward effort, even if it doesn't meet your standards of hygiene! If she feels you approve of her attempts, she's much more likely to continue them.

4   Keep the situation in perspective. Kids with messy rooms are no more likely to become criminals than anyone else and, in the end, they are the ones who have to live in it. If it drives you crazy, close the door and don't look. Even the most untidy child will be driven to create a little order at some point.

5   For older children, make it clear that clothes that don't make it to the laundry bin don't get washed. They'll soon twig, particularly if their underwear drawer is empty.

6   You can make cleaning and tidying their rooms a weekly routine. Give them a list of what needs to be done and get them to tick it off as they go. Don't be too fussy when you come to check. If they have made an effort and done at least some of everything on the list, let them go.

What Children Learn

Everyone needs to learn that it's impossible to operate in complete chaos and that they are, ultimately, responsible for their own environment. Teach them the ropes and then show faith in them. They'll eventually take pride in their own space and want to keep it reasonably neat.

Maintenance

If you have trouble maintaining a cleaning routine, get the star charts out and reward efforts to keep things neat. Invite some of their friends round. There is nothing more embarrassing than being caught out and you may encourage them to undertake a superfast tidy in order to save face. You may offer to redecorate, in order to provide them with a clean slate. Let them become involved in the proceedings so that they feel that their room is their own space. Get rid of the clutter, get a good, serviceable wastepaper basket and laundry bin and then see what happens. You may find you have a pack rat extraordinaire on your hands and nothing you do will ever change that. In which case, take heart. If you can keep it clean enough to prevent the health authorities from visiting, just shut the door and remember that eventually they will be someone else's problem.

Complaining

Children complain for all sorts of different reasons. The crux of the problem, most of the time, is that they feel a sense of injustice which they don't think you have recognized.

What to Do

1   Remember that everyone complains from time to time. It's one way of expressing discontent without causing too much trouble. But for parents, it can be enormously exhausting and, as the backdrop to family life, unbelievably irritating. The first thing you need to do is listen – actively. Let them get off their chest whatever is troubling them and don't belittle their moans. Show them that you have heard them and that their feelings are valid and understandable. But then, ensure that you focus on solving the problem. Say: 'I can see your point, but moaning about it isn't going to help, is it? What do you think we can do to change things?'

2   Make sure your child is given enough attention. A great deal of complaining has to do with perceived inequality. Find out what he thinks he needs and see if you can find a way to satisfy that.

3   Make sure you don't give in to complaining. Your child may have developed an unhealthy habit of thinking he'll get what he wants by moaning. And he may be right. You may wish to do anything to ensure that he shuts up.

4   Look at your own behaviour. Do you complain constantly? If so, you have set an example that your child will undoubtedly follow. Try to look more positively at situations, and seek resolutions rather than bemoaning your fate. Be optimistic and show your children an ability to see the bright side, to negotiate change and to solve problems.

5   Give your children a time limit. If they follow you around complaining, turn to them and say that you are willing to give them three more minutes to get it off their chest and then you expect to hear solutions and positive steps forward rather than wallowing.

6   Verbalize their feelings. Say, 'I know you are disappointed/frustrated/angry/upset/sad, and I feel that way too when things don't go my way.' Then

show them that action is much more effective than self-pity.

7 Remember that complaining is an avoidance skill, and something you do not want to encourage in your child. He needs to learn to be proactive, and that he is the only one who has control over his destiny. To that end, offer choices. Show faith in his decision-making (even when he makes mistakes). Believe that he can make changes towards his wellbeing, and generally empower him so that he learns to believe in his own ability to find solutions.

What Children Learn

They learn that complaining ultimately gets them nowhere and that the only way to see change is to make it themselves. They also learn that a complainer is not much fun to be around, and that the whole family/friendship dynamic is much livelier, healthier and proactive when the emphasis is on action rather than moaning. They'll also learn that life can be disappointing at times, and that we don't always get what we want.

Maintenance

Try to find a middle ground with your children. Those who grow up in an over-permissive environment tend to believe that they should get what they want, no matter what. And they'll use whatever means to hand to get there. Similarly, over-controlled children become either overly willing to please, or they rebel. Complaining is a form of rebellion because it shows an inability to move forward and seek out solutions, no matter how good they might be. Give your children some power, show no tolerance for complaining without cause, and continue to encourage problem-solving.

Demanding

Demanding children are used to getting their own way. They have not learned to respect the family rules or approach to living. Punishment does not help a demanding child, nor does giving in. What you need to do is ensure they do not expect to have their demands fulfilled. That starts with a firm approach to discipline and parenting.

What to Do

1   Don't give in to petty demands ('I don't like that glass'; 'I want coke, not blackcurrant'; 'I want a different toy'). If you do so once, they'll continue to demand. They've got you over a barrel and they know it. In the end, they've got your full attention, something every child craves.

2   Offer choices in advance, to prevent indecision later. 'Do you want the blue cup or the red mug?'; 'Do you want blackcurrant, water or orange juice?'; 'Do you want Buzz Lightyear or the dog for the car journey?' If they feel empowered to make choices, they'll learn a little self-respect. They are also in no position to argue later.

3   Show children how to take on general responsibilities themselves: how to get their own drinks, shoes, snacks, videos, etc. No parent needs to be a slave to their children. If you teach them early on that they need to take some responsibility, they are less likely to demand that you do.

4   Be very clear when you will be available to help your child. If you are busy with the laundry or a phone call, work or even reading the paper, you can justifiably say that this is not the right time and that you will be ready in X number of minutes. You may

meet some resistance at the outset, but stay firm. Children need to respect your time.

What Children Learn

They learn that demanding things gets them nowhere. Instead, negotiation can be undertaken, or they are more likely to get what they want if they do it themselves. This doesn't mean you are a negligent parent; it simply involves your child learning to take responsibility for some aspects of her life. If you remain calm, kind and firm, your child will learn that love does not equate to getting whatever she wants. You will convey that it is possible for her to solve problems herself.

Maintenance

In busy periods, your determination may falter and you may find yourself giving in, or resorting to punishment. Go back to square one. Explain what you feel your child can do herself, and make it clear that once she has made a decision (based on choices), there is no going back. You are not going to be a slave and the best way to get your attention is to be prepared to share a little fun and interaction.

Depression

Depression is a prolonged feeling of unhappiness and despondency, often magnified by a major life event such as bereavement or parental divorce. Many children and adolescents suffer from depression, which can also be the result of fluctuating hormones or undue stress. It can also follow a viral illness, such as glandular fever.

If your child is depressed, try to remember that it is an illness and they won't just 'snap out of it'. It's important to be patient and to spend as much time as you can boosting

self-confidence and self-respect (*see page 68*) and helping
your child to feel good about himself, even in the depths
of despair.

Some common signs of depression include:

- poor concentration
- irritability
- loss of self-esteem
- insomnia and early-morning waking
- loss of appetite
- feelings of emptiness or despair

What to Do

1   First of all, don't be embarrassed or proud about
    seeking help. Most depression is caused by chemical
    imbalances in the brain, or other physical or
    emotional reasons. It is not a reflection of poor
    parenting skills. You child may well need a bit of
    counselling, or some complementary or orthodox
    medical treatment. Don't rule it out. It can make all
    the difference. Similarly, however, don't count on
    drugs to sort out your child's problems. Depression
    can indicate deep issues that need to be resolved and
    it is your responsibility as a parent to get to the bottom
    of it.

2   Remember that everyone – children included –
    experiences depression from time to time. It may be a
    sign that something disturbing is happening in their
    lives. You will need to spend plenty of time opening
    the communication channels in order to work out
    what that might be.

3   Don't assume that you know why your child is
    depressed or unhappy. Ask open-ended questions
    about what's going on, such as 'I can see you are
    feeling a bit gloomy, is there anything I can do to

help?', or 'Is there something happening in your life that is making you feel sad?'

4   Ensure they don't feel frightened or confused by their feelings. Explain that it is normal to feel unhappy from time to time, and help them find the words to describe how they are feeling.

5   Many children become low when they feel they are not good enough, or are failing to live up to expectations. Ensure that your child feels good about himself. Let him know that he is loved unconditionally, no matter how he performs in other areas of his life.

6   Focus on the positive in your child's life. Point out all the good things he has and does. Help him see that even periods of deep unhappiness can be overcome if he asks for help. Teach him that all clouds have silver linings.

What Children Learn

All of us need to learn that feeling unhappy or gloomy is a part of life, and that there is always a light at the end of the tunnel. Children learn to ask for help when they are feeling depressed, and see that talking things through can relieve a great deal of the burden. They also learn to look for the positive in their lives and ride the bad periods more easily.

Maintenance

If there is a regular, deep-seated problem, you will need to seek some external help. For irregular bursts of depression, try to be understanding. Hormones play crazy tricks on a child's mind and outlook and little problems at school or elsewhere can build up to the point where they appear insurmountable. The best thing you can do is keep the channels of communication open so that you have a good idea of what is going on in your child's life. Show unconditional love and offer practical solutions for getting through difficult periods.

Destruction

Most children are not destructive by nature, although they can be clumsy and cause all sorts of catastrophes accidentally. They may also become destructive through boredom or simply because it seemed like a fun idea at the time (*see page 114*). But children who regularly destroy things, either to punish you or as an act of revenge, need to learn respect for their environment and for the household rules.

What to Do

1   If damage is accidental, involve your child in the clearing up, but ensure you don't lay blame or apply punishments. Accidents happen. It's equally important to make sure you aren't too precious about your home. Kids make a mess, they break things and they are, generally, untidy. Lower your expectations, or find a room where they can be children without the worry of causing you displeasure.

2   If the damage is playful, explain why the destruction of property is unacceptable and make sure they clear it away. Ask why they undertook the behaviour. If they were bored, make suggestions for other activities. You don't necessarily need to punish a child for making a genuine mistake (if she *genuinely* didn't know it was wrong), but you do need to show her how to rectify it.

3   Wilful damage needs to be nipped in the bud. Teach your children alternative forms of expressing anger and discontent. Make them responsible for their

actions by asking them to pay for a proportion of any damage caused, such as through their pocket money on a weekly basis. They'll have a regular reminder of this particular lesson for some weeks to come.

4 Encourage them to take pride in possessions. Let them become involved in decorating their own rooms and choosing their things. Don't let them grow up thinking that everything is replaceable. If they break something, don't replace it. Let them learn that they aren't the only ones who suffer by this type of behaviour.

5 Make destruction of property a big no-no on the family rule list. At the outset, explain why it is unnecessary, hurtful and counterproductive.

What Children Learn

They learn to respect other people's possessions and belongings and to take pride in their own, as well as seeing that there are alternative ways of expressing fury. They will learn to accept the value of money if their pocket money is docked to pay for damage, and will definitely think twice before repeating the action. And if they are involved in the clean-up (which is unlikely to be anything other than boring), they may wish to discontinue such actions altogether.

Maintenance

If destructive behaviour begins again, you will need to work out why your child is expressing herself in this manner. Open up the lines of communication. Encourage her to verbalize her feelings. Be understanding and then embark on some problem-solving sessions. If children learn to cope with things in different ways, they will learn an invaluable life skill.

Discontent

It's a natural childhood ailment to feel some discontent, particularly when there is clear inequality in the way people bring up their children and choose to treat them. There is a certain amount of peer pressure involved in this type of discontent, as children often think they need to match their peers with possessions and freedom in order to be popular. Younger children simply have a voracious appetite for possessions of any nature, fed largely by television and other media.

What to Do

1   First, you need to ensure your child feels valuable and worthy in his own right and that he understands that possessions or freedom do not make someone popular. It is acceptable to adjust your view of what is permissible freedom to fall more in line with the majority of his peers. We can all be guilty of being overprotective and it's worth asking around to see what other parents feel. There's nothing worse than being a teenaged leper. However, your child does need to learn that your rules are there for a reason, and that a lot of possessions do not necessarily show love or indeed good parenting. Although this can be a tough lesson to get across, giving in will teach your child nothing. He won't learn the value of money, or the fact that a loving parent is worth a lot more than a few possessions or some inappropriate freedom. He won't understand that there are always boundaries in our lives that need to be maintained, however much we disagree with them.

2   Ensure your child has a strong sense of self and an understanding of the way things work in your family. If you explain things clearly, he can then explain his position to others.

3   Bolster his self-respect. Give him choices about what is purchased for him (within limits) and give him power and responsibility in other ways, so that he feels good about himself.

4   Insecure children feel they can bolster their self-image and make up for any perceived inadequacies by 'blending in' – having the same things as their friends and doing what they do. Find activities at which he will shine and where he will make friends with like-minded children. This will give him an area of his life where he stands out and feels important. Work on making him feel good for being who he is – 'You have such a great sense of humour', 'You look so handsome in that shirt', 'You worked hard for that result (good or not).'

5   Children do need to learn the value of money and realize that material goods are not the answer. Find and point out kids who are popular without the 'gear' and see if you can find some who have it all and have not achieved 'status'. Then negotiate a compromise. Agree on one or two new things during a specific time space. This will help him focus on what he really does want, rather than what he 'must' have. If he wants more, he'll have to earn the money to buy it by getting a paper round, for example, or baby-sitting or helping out around the house. This will help to teach him the value of money and make his possessions more valuable because he has earned them. One or two small 'in' things will help him feel normal.

6   In terms of freedom, you can, again, negotiate a compromise, but once you have made a decision, stick with it (*see page 18*). It will be tricky at first, but your child will eventually respect your position and kick up fewer fusses as time goes on.

7   Younger children can be given choices when the decision to purchase a new toy crops up. In this way they will feel satisfied that they have had some power and a say in the matter. It's likely to take some time for them to understand that they can't have everything they want, but be firm. Gently remind them of the toys and games they do have, and get them out. Better still, keep some away from the playroom for a period of time and then swap them over. They'll feel like they have a whole new selection to choose from.

What Children Learn

Simply that there are always inequalities in life and that we may never get what we want. Teach them that the grass is always greener, and that some of these 'cool' kids may well lack some of the wonderful things your child has, such as respect, genuine regard for his wellbeing, a happy family dynamic and trust. He'll also see that material possessions are not the key to happiness or fitting in (the more he has, the more he will be likely to want and the less satisfied he will feel), but that those purchased through hard work, and carefully chosen, can be much more rewarding.

Maintenance

Keep tabs on what your children's friends are doing. While there is absolutely no point in joining in the competition, you want to ensure you are being realistic in your expectations and in what you are willing to buy for your child. I remember once being on a school trip with my eldest son. Every single child had Pokémon cards, bar one, whose parents didn't believe in it. They seemed, to me, to be speaking another language altogether, and this one child was completely isolated. This type of parental resolve is nonsensical. Remember that popular culture plays an important role in the lives of today's children, and they will need to feel part of that to some degree. For the non-essentials, however, stick to your guns. Explain, negotiate and compromise where necessary, but continue to encourage self-respect in your child so that he simply has far less need for these things.

Drugs and Alcohol

This subject deserves a book on its own and I cannot do it full justice with one entry. However, it's worth remembering that children seek drugs or alcohol for much the same reason that we might – escape from the troubles of daily life, peer pressure and fitting in, natural experimentation and even just boredom. The problem is, of course, that it can become habit and lead to dependency, which is exactly what needs to be avoided.

Signs of Drug Abuse

When children start using drugs, they usually exhibit many different signs which parents need to watch out for. Unfortunately, many parents often write off these signs as normal adolescent behaviour. As a result, they don't realize that there is a problem until it is too late. Keep an eye out for the signs. If you have a close relationship, it should become immediately clear.

- dramatic changes in style of clothes, hair, music
- being late going to or coming home from school and/or truancies
- lack of motivation in school
- isolation from the family
- changes in attitude and personality
- changes in sleep patterns
- sudden over- or undereating

- paranoia
- dilated, red or glazed eyes
- sudden bursts of anger
- lying
- dramatic mood swings
- suddenly spending a great deal of money; or you notice money disappearing
- talking too slow or too fast

What to Do

1 First of all, ensure your child has a full and happy life so she does not feel the need to fill it with recreational substances. A recent study showed that children who are involved in music, for example, are far less likely to resort to drugs. I suspect that is because they are simply too busy to find the time and too stimulated to have the need.

2 Empower your child and ensure she has a healthy self-respect (*see page 68*). Peer pressure is then less likely to become such an issue.

3 Educate your child about the dangers of drugs and alcohol in a reasonable way. Scare tactics rarely work, but if you spell it out in a relevant way she's more likely to listen – 'You won't be able to attain your goal of being an athlete/getting a scholarship/making the netball squad if you damage your heart, liver and mind.' Don't be unrealistic. There are undoubted pleasures and an element of relaxation involved in drinking. In a child who is less confident, the idea of losing inhibitions can be extremely tempting. Explain that you understand the appeal, but the dangers are ...

4 If your child does confess to trying drugs, don't go overboard with fury. The most important thing you can do with an adolescent is to keep the

communication flowing. You want her to be able to confide in you without fear of recrimination, and she needs to know you love her, no matter what mistakes she makes. That doesn't mean being accepting of things you disapprove of; it simply means saying something along the lines of: 'Thank you for confiding in me. I value your honesty.' Then lead into a conversation where you can express your concerns and she can discuss the motivation for trying. If it was experimental, you will have to accept that this is a normal part of growing up. Just remind her of her goals in life and show your faith in her ability to make the right decisions in future.

5   If you find that your child is regularly taking drugs, try not to panic. Show faith in her ability to change course but be determined to find out the motivation for this type of behaviour. Is she under pressure from her friends? Is there a hole in her life that needs filling? Does she feel unable to cope? Show your unconditional support and love by helping her through and working together to find a solution for any problems she may be experiencing in her life.

6   If you suspect your child has a drug problem she is keeping from you, seek professional help. It's almost impossible to deal with problems of this nature alone, and you want to be sure to get it right.

7   Watch your own use of drugs and alcohol. If you regularly use alcohol to relax or to enable you to have fun, your children are likely to follow suit. You have, in essence, made it acceptable. Similarly, if you rely on pills for everything from headaches and sleep problems to feeling low, your children will see that they are acceptable (albeit in a more legal form!).

8   Talk to your children early on (from about age 11 onwards) about the difference between doing things

in moderation and going overboard. Let them learn how to moderate their own behaviour – doing homework for set periods of time; turning off the television or games consoles after an agreed period; and avoiding overindulgence in general, whether it is eating sweets or drinking too many cans of coke.

9   From an early age, encourage your children to think about what might be the results of alcohol or drug addiction. Invite them to use their imaginations and think it through. For example, you might ask: 'What kind of life do you think someone has if they are addicted to drugs?' and then 'What do you want your life to be like?' Ask them if they have ever seen a drunk on the street, and to imagine what it might be like to be that person. If they can think through the potential dangers and problems, and picture it in their minds, they are more likely to want to resist it. This works a lot better than lecturing ever will.

What Children Learn

Your child will learn that she has a non-judgmental, loving family to whom she can turn when things go wrong. If she can talk to you without fearing punishment, she will not feel so frightened and alone, and she will be much more likely to resist the pressure to become involved in things she does not believe in.

Maintenance

Watch for signs of abuse of drugs or alcohol (*see above*) and don't hesitate to engage your child in conversation. Avoid confrontations and anger or punishment. What you need is an open, honest relationship where you can both share your concerns. If you are too judgmental, you'll drive the problem underground and then you have no means to help. Keep your kids busy and keep tabs on their level of wellbeing. Happy kids are much less likely to go off the rails. Spend regular time with your children. You will never be able to pick up the signs if you aren't around to do so.

Eating

Faddy eating is something that drives parents to distraction, and it's not surprising. As parents, we are responsible for our children's health, and there is nothing more worrying than a child who resists all attempts to eat good, nutritious food. What's more, because mealtimes tend to fall when we are least able to cope (during the rush to get to school or at the end of the day when we are tired and pressured), children often learn that being difficult will win them that much-desired attention, whether it is negative or not.

What to Do

1 Early in life, most children cotton on to the fact that their parents are concerned about how much and what they are eating. Making a fuss about food guarantees instant attention, and many children slide into the habit of using food to wield power over their parents. Other children are simply not interested in food, and the concerted efforts of their parents to make them eat put them off even further. For parents of all picky eaters, the best advice is to remove the pressure. If children fail to get a response, they get bored. If they realize they won't get attention for eating badly, they'll stop using food as a tool to do so. If the pressure is off at the dinner table, children will start developing a healthier attitude to food – it's there to eat. It's neither poison nor a miracle medicine. Food can be enjoyed when it is not associated with parental nagging.

2   Don't make a fuss at mealtimes. There will be times when your child is starving and will demolish anything in sight. At other times, he will pick and graze and seem to need nothing substantial. Go with the flow. Never force a child to clear his plate. He'll grow up associating food with stress and bad behaviour. The clean plate brigade was disarmed a long time ago.

3   Children need to learn to recognize when they are hungry and when they are full. Ultimately, they will learn self-control and self-regulation. If you decide when they are full for them, they'll never learn when to stop. That doesn't mean giving children free rein. If your child genuinely doesn't like something – mushrooms, for example – don't force it. Suggest that he tries one bite. Or if he's not very hungry, suggest three bites of everything on the plate. Children need to learn to try foods and they need to eat a variety of good foods in order to stay healthy.

4   Show some respect. We all have foods we don't like and there are healthy eaters who simply cannot abide a particular vegetable, meat or flavour. Don't force a child to eat food he dislikes. The problem with faddy eaters, of course, is that they claim not to like anything. That's a different scenario. If your child eats well, tries new things and eats a healthy, varied diet, then the odd 'no-way' food can be dropped from the daily diet. But don't give up. Try new recipes. Introduce it again in a month's time. Children's tastes change, and what may have been considered revolting one week may be the new favourite later on. If your child rejects a food after trying it a number of times, and continues to dislike it despite your best efforts, leave it for a period of time.

5   Don't buy what you don't want your child to eat. If you have a cupboard full of crisps and biscuits and a

refrigerator full of processed foods, you are fighting a losing battle. If there are alternatives to hand, you are unlikely to convince a child that he should eat what's put in front of him – particularly if he knows that you will cave in later and allow an inappropriate snack. Make a concerted effort to change the eating habits of the whole family, and start by running down the junk food. If your child will only eat chicken nuggets, don't buy them. If he fills up on crisps, leave them on the supermarket shelves. If there is nothing else, children will eat what's put in front of them.

6   Along the same lines, don't offer alternatives. Serve a healthy meal for the whole family and don't panic if your child doesn't eat much. If he is hungry, he will eat. Even the most resolute child will not starve himself to death.

7   Educate your child. Explain what foods are healthy and what they do for our bodies. Children love information, and they'll feel important if you take the time to explain things. Don't assume that they won't be interested. That doesn't mean boring them with facts about vitamins and minerals. Make it relevant – if you have a sportsman, point out that unrefined carbohydrates will give him more energy for the big match. If he's got a cold, explain that fresh fruits and vegetables have lots of vitamin C, which will help his cold go away.

8   Don't label your child. Parents often create self-fulfilling prophecies. If a child thinks he's picky, he will be. If you continually praise your child during meals for what he does eat, and insist to everyone around that your child is such a good eater, he'll take some pride in this achievement.

9   Empower your child. If he feels he's lost control, he'll dig in his heels or revert to tears or tantrums. Make

up a list of eight or nine good, healthy meals, with a variety of different vegetables on the side. Let each child in the family choose a particular night's menu. You can suggest that there have to be at least four fruits or vegetables with every meal, and at least two have to be different from the meal chosen for the previous night. If you make it into a game, children will be more likely to become involved. They'll also feel that they have some control.

10 Involve your children in preparing and cooking food. Even very young children can help in some way, even if it is just stirring or adding ingredients. Ask a vegetable phobic to make the salad. Offer heaps of praise with the result. If they made it, they'll feel proud of it and they'll be more likely to eat it.

11 Introduce new foods alongside the old favourites, and then slowly drop the parts of your child's diet that concern you most. Don't be tempted to launch a dramatically different eating programme overnight. You'll incite mutiny! Instead, make small changes. Every new food your child eats is a step in the right direction.

12 Introduce a star chart or the equivalent. Children can be encouraged to put a star up for every healthy or new food they eat. When they reach an agreed total, you can offer a reward.

13 Place the serving dishes on the table and encourage children to help themselves. They'll naturally choose more of the things they like, but as long as they eat a little of everything, they can be allowed to make choices about quantity.

14 If your child refuses food or just picks at his food for a long time, don't push it. Don't make him feel guilty if he's just not hungry, and don't ever make him eat to

please you. This sort of emotional blackmail can lower your child's self-respect and make him insecure.

15 Eat the same foods as your children. There should be no distinction between children's food and adult food. Good, healthy food is appropriate for the whole family. If children see their parents enjoying a broad range of foods, they'll be more likely to try some.

16 Eat with your children. If they see you eating the same things they are eating, they will feel reassured. Like anyone else, children enjoy company. If they are faced with a solitary supper, they'll probably not be very interested. Make mealtimes fun with lots of conversation or laughter.

What Children Learn

All children need to learn to eat healthily and to enjoy good, wholesome food. As you expand their diets, they'll learn to appreciate things and take pleasure at mealtimes. They'll also learn that you aren't going to give in to their tricks to get your attention. They'll see that mealtimes can be fun and that there is plenty of time for communication and laughter if the hassles die down.

Maintenance

Once children begin to eat well, problems normally only crop up when they are overtired, ill or under pressure. Look for the causes, and don't assume that the behaviour has taken a backslide. All of us have times when we are not hungry. Remember that. Ensure that you keep mealtimes fun and light-hearted. Don't focus too heavily on manners or expectations, and remember to avoid confrontations or arguing, whatever the cost. If your child begins to associate mealtimes with yet another 'go' at him, he'll become reluctant to join in.

Fears

Never underestimate your child's concerns or fears. There may be a serious problem at school affecting her emotional health, or something simple may have affected her more dramatically than perhaps it should have done. Whether or not you consider a problem to be valid is irrelevant. If it is enough to cause your child to become upset, and to manifest physical symptoms, something has to be done about it.

What to Do

1   The most important thing you can do is get to the bottom of it. Spend as much time as you can with your child talking things through. It may be that she is too traumatized or upset to talk about it, or she may be vaguely embarrassed or ashamed of her concerns. She may not even be able to pinpoint what the problem is – there may just be a general feeling of unhappiness and fear, or self-consciousness. Choose different times of the day for chats, and use personal examples to lead into discussions. For example, you could recount a childhood experience that upset you greatly. Children respond well to comparisons because it helps them believe that they are not weird or unusual.

2   Talk to your child's teacher and, if necessary, other classmates to find out if there is anything driving the fear at school. Are there problems at home with another sibling or between you and your partner? Express your own concerns and emotions. This will help your child see that what she feels is normal.

3   Validate her feelings by letting her know that everyone feels frightened at some time or another. The way through is to think positively, face the fears

and understand what is driving them, and to find ways to relax enough to get through difficult periods. It sometimes helps to imagine the worst possible scenario for a frightening situation. If she works her way through this mentally, she may find it isn't as difficult as it might seem.

4   If your child is afraid of something tangible, such as dogs or spiders, verify her feelings: 'You are afraid because they might bite you and you just want them to go away.' Sometimes just having feelings validated lessens the fear.

5   Help them to find ways through fearful situations, without actually trying to fix it yourself. Ask them if having a light at night or a teddy would help a fear of the dark, or if they would prefer to have the dog in their friend's house, on a lead or in another room. Give them some choices so that they feel in control of the situation.

6   Don't ever force children into situations that frighten them simply to prove that they can do it or that they are 'brave'. Small steps are a much better idea. Looking at dogs in books, for example, then on a video. Then petting a small, child-friendly dog. Let her see other children reacting to the problem situation with confidence – swimming, if your child is afraid of water; playing with a dog in the park, if dogs are a fear; chasing insects, etc.

7   Show faith that your child can get through it. If she has even a seed in her mind that it is surmountable, she's well on the way to recovery.

What Children Learn

Children learn that it's acceptable and normal to feel fear, but that it doesn't need to take over their lives to the point where they are overwhelmed by it. They also learn that they have courage within them to overcome fears, which will give them strength in the future.

Maintenance

Try not to assume that because your child has successfully overcome a fear on a single instance that the problem is solved. Continue to show faith in her ability to confront fears and work out her motivation for them. Respect your child's differences and don't feel that you have somehow failed as a parent. Dealing with fears is a life experience that will stand them in good stead in the future.

Fighting with Family

Fighting or arguing is commonplace in many families. It can be driven by sibling rivalry (*see page 226*) or simply frustration and anger. Children may feel a sense of injustice and believe that their only recourse is to fight. They may also feel hurt and want to hurt someone back. Remember, however, that it takes two people to have an argument, and if one of you fails to rise to the bait, it simply won't take place. Arguing can be enormously satisfying for a child because he can express his emotions, get things off his chest and usually, in the heat of the moment, tell you or another family member exactly what he thinks. The end result is, however, rarely pleasant, and children can feel insecure (as if they may have tested you beyond the radius of your love), guilty, frightened by their own rage and equally frightened by yours.

What to Do

1 Make it a family policy to avoid arguments and fights. They are bound to happen, but if everyone aims towards a positive goal, it shows willing.
2 Model appropriate behaviour. If you have a

tempestuous relationship with your partner and your child hears or sees you regularly fighting or arguing, he is more likely to see it as a way of dealing with problems.

3   Don't be drawn into a slanging match. It's all too easy, when we are insulted or accosted by an angry child, to join in. After all, pride is at stake, as is our authority. But children need reassurance, not angry words. They need to know that you love them, despite their angry feelings, and that you are prepared to help them find alternative methods of expressing their anger (*see page 92*).

4   Help them to verbalize their feelings. Arguments often occur when a child (or adult) feels that things have built up to bursting point, and he needs to air his views. Listen carefully to his perceived grievances. They may seem trite or unimportant, but they have clearly combined to mean a lot to your child. Respect his feelings and help him see that it's easier to talk small problems through than it is to wait until they have built up and grown into something significant.

5   Defuse the situation with humour. When faced with an irate, shouting child, make him laugh by saying something silly. Then you can sit down and talk rationally.

6   Above all, encourage your children not to hold grudges. When a fight or argument is over, it's over. There's no point in harking back to past grievances. Far better to look forward to better ways of doing things.

What Children Learn

They learn that fighting inevitably leads to negative feelings, and can increase the tension rather than clear the air. They also learn that there are other ways to solve problems besides fighting and that you love them whether they have angry feelings or not. This helps them to feel comfortable talking to you and airing even negative feelings, which is a positive step forward for a healthy relationship.

Fighting with Friends

Arguments with friends are part of growing up. Although it can be painful for a parent to witness, it is something children need to learn to sort out themselves – with your love and support. Remember that children overcome slights a lot more easily than adults, and move on (often with the same friends) as if nothing has happened. Don't be tempted to protect your child from this experience, or to intervene, as instinct may dictate.

What to Do

1   Once again, it's important to ensure that your child is witness to healthy interaction in your household. If they see you negotiating, problem-solving as a unit (or a couple), co-operating and showing understanding, they are much more likely to use these skills in their own relationships.

2   Show understanding of their feelings – anger, betrayal, fear that they may have lost a friend, frustration or pain. It may be that your child makes it up with her friend, but equally she may not. People do fall out, but children can learn that it's possible to experience pain, get over it and move on. If your children feel they can confide in you, and that their feelings are validated, it may be enough to defuse the situation. They feel they have some support, even if it isn't where it is most required.

3 Offer support, but don't try to solve the problem for them. Show faith in their ability to work it out themselves. Let them know you are there if they need you.

4 Don't show too much pity. The last thing your child needs is to feel like a victim.

5 Don't push your children to make things up or to see friends with whom they have fallen out. You may not fully understand the reasons why your child called a halt to things. She will resume the relationship if and when she is ready. By the same token, however, encourage forgiveness and humility. No one gains if pride prevents them from getting something they really want.

What Children Learn

All children need to experience the ups and downs of relationships, and find ways within themselves to cope with the pain and other emotions that accompany these swings. Fighting with friends teaches them skills that will be with them for life. They will learn to negotiate, to forgive, to cooperate and to divert their anger. They also learn that you are there for them, as a sounding board and a sympathetic, loving parent, but that there are times in their lives when they need to call upon their own resources.

Maintenance

Stay out of your children's relationships as much as possible. Be a sympathetic listener, and show unconditional love and faith, but always allow them to sort things out themselves.

Forgetting

Children forget things because:

- their minds are swirling with new and exciting information that is being processed as they grow up
- their lives and their bodies are changing constantly
- they are, today, under excessive pressure from various sources (parental expectations, exams, over-scheduling, etc.)
- they simply do not have the same priorities as us

We may think it's important – crucial, even – for a child to remember his games bag in the morning and to bring home his instrument or the correct books for homework at the end of the day. He, however, probably has his mind on 'greater' things, such as who to trade the newest collector's cards with, or what's on television that evening, or who's fallen out with who at school.

What to Do

1 Show a little patience. All of us have the potential to forget things, particularly when we are stressed or busy. And it is often the less important things that slip through the net.

2 If your child constantly forgets or loses articles of clothing, for example, you may be driven to the point of despair. Don't be tempted, however, to continually replace lost items. Show concern and sympathy, but let him see that if he loses something he won't have it until he finds it or replaces it himself. It may teach him to be a little more careful at the outset. Rescuing your child continually will not solve the problem.

3 From an early age, try to encourage your children to take responsibility for their own belongings. If you do

everything for them and constantly remind them, they'll learn to rely on you and never really take it seriously.

4   If your child continually forgets his homework, there may be an issue you need to address. Perhaps he is battling with his teacher about something and wishes to make a point; maybe he feels you are overly involved in his homework and he doesn't want that pressure. Maybe he lacks the belief that he can do the homework. Ask some questions. Find out the truth and help your child find ways to solve the problem himself.

5   Make things easy. Put a checklist on the front door which he can survey on his way out of the house. Encourage him to write a schedule of what is required to come home from school each day and put it at the front of his school bag. He may not use it, but he will then have no real excuse or argument.

6   'I forget' also seems to be another way of saying 'I don't care', or 'I don't want to'. Try to encourage your children to tell you the truth of the matter. Ask leading questions until you get to the root of the problem.

7   If forgetfulness is a real problem, put it on your list of family rules and come to some agreement. Rewards for things remembered, but penalties for things repeatedly forgotten. Eventually the penny will drop if you can find a way to motivate him to remember.

What Children Learn

Organization, keeping track of property and the art of writing lists, schedules or reminders in order to keep all of the balls in the air. You can guide this process, but ultimately they need to learn these skills themselves, through trial and error. The inconvenience of going without things (which may get them into trouble at school) may be enough to shift the emphasis and encourage them to view these things as important, rather than something you will rectify later on.

Maintenance

Children can become more forgetful when they are under pressure or when they have a lot on their minds. Be patient through these periods, and start a new system – lists, reminders or anything else that will help to jog their memories.

Friends (what to do if you don't approve)

Children will choose their own friends whether we like it or not. Trying to manipulate that choice will only end up undermining your own relationship with your child. It may be that the friends with whom your children keep company are what you would consider to be a bad influence. It may also be that you wish your child was more popular, and hanging out with the 'right' crowd. This may sound silly, but many parents subconsciously live through their children and hope to see them as part of the 'cool' group or the 'A' students, the music maestros or the athletes.

What to Do

1   Show trust and assume that your child's choice of friends is right for her. If you feel that negative characteristics of one or more friend may lead your child astray, ensure they are welcome in your home and use your own positive relationship with your child to balance things.

2   Remember that every child is unique and an individual. What you think is right for her probably

isn't, and she will feel happiest in the company of friends she chooses. It may be that your child's lifestyle will never live up to your expectations, but that is something you are going to have to accept.

3 Don't worry if your child doesn't seem to be 'popular'. Some people are comfortable with one or two best friends; others feel happier in big groups. Whatever the case, your child will only ever be popular with her friends if she feels good about herself. If you make her feel inadequate in any way, she will become insecure and less able to sustain lasting and valuable friendships.

4 If your child has difficulty making friends, help her by encouraging a variety of different activities, where she is more likely to meet people with whom she has something in common. Don't make her feel pressured. If it is something that concerns her, listen, validate her concerns and make her feel confident about her abilities so that when the opportunity does crop up, she'll be able to make use of it.

5 Don't use subversive tactics to try to change your children's friendships. They'll soon cotton on to what you are doing and sense your disapproval. This not only undermines their confidence and leads them to believe they are not capable of choosing or attracting the 'right' friends, but it lowers their self-respect.

6 Ensure your child feels she 'fits in' to some degree. If you impose your ideas about the way she should dress, act and what she should have in her lifestyle, she may feel embarrassed or believe she has no sense of identity. Give her some choices about the way she lives her life (within safe boundaries).

What Children Learn

They learn to be independent and that their choices are acceptable to the people who matter most – their family. Your child will also see that her family is always there and loves her unconditionally, which is a great foundation for confidence and self-respect. From this springboard she will go out into the world feeling sure of herself and her self-worth and likeability.

Maintenance

As your child becomes older, continue to welcome her friends and show approval. There may be someone you consider to be a 'bad egg' on the scene occasionally, but show faith in your child to make the right decisions (*see also 'Peers', page 51*).

Getting Dressed

This is a problem for little ones more than older children (although you may have a comfort bunny who likes to stay in his pyjamas all day long). The solution is simple: give choices.

What to Do

1   If your child resists getting dressed in the morning, he is choosing the opportune time to wind you up. He knows he has to, he knows you are going to make him, so why not make the most of the situation? Empower your child. Say: 'Do you want to get dressed now or after breakfast?' 'Do you want to wear your red socks or your blue ones?' Do this for every article of clothing until you have your child's perfect outfit to hand. This may sound time-consuming, but it prevents the inevitable battle.

2 Do this the night before, if there isn't enough time in the morning. A little pre-planning goes a long way.

3 Make a family rule that everyone has to be dressed before breakfast (with exceptions, such as weekends) or before the television goes on (during weekends or holidays, for example). The rule is that it has to happen. Reward successes and use the warning system if it goes wrong.

4 Get your child a watch with an alarm. Even small children will learn that when the beeping starts, it's time to put on their clothes. This is learned behaviour and it is remarkably effective. It works particularly well because they are given some responsibility and it makes them feel important.

5   If they repeatedly fail to get dressed on time, suggest
    they go to school in their pyjamas, and look like you
    intend to fulfil this warning. Or, from time to time,
    leave them behind. It only takes one missed
    opportunity for fun (self-caused) for a child to realize
    that you mean business.

What Children Learn

To make choices within a time scale and to organize their
time and their clothing to meet deadlines. They also learn
that you aren't going to rise to the bait and argue with them.

Maintenance

Make sure you aren't putting too much pressure on your
child to be ready too quickly. Give yourself lots of time,
but make it clear what you expect. If it slips, get the star
charts out again.

Holidays

Holidays are a bit like birthdays – they hold the promise
of dreams and wishes coming true. The reality is, however,
sometimes much bleaker. If you are away, the weather
might be diabolical and scupper all your plans. Children
may also resent the fact that you need a break and are not
willing to be at their beck and call all day long. Things
such as discipline can also slip out of control when
the routine shifts. Even if they are at home during the
holidays, the structure of their day has been altered and
they may feel unsettled.

What to Do

1   Set in place a holiday routine, which will help to
    structure your children's time and let them know
    what to expect and when.

2 Don't be tempted to let the television, video or computer do the baby-sitting for you. The children will end up becoming wound up and their behaviour will slide.

3 Try to keep bedtimes realistic. This can be done by offering your children a limited choice in advance: 'Would you like to go to bed half an hour or an hour later now that the holidays have begun?' The same thing goes for games consoles and computers: 'I'm willing to alter the rules for the holidays, so do you want an extra hour a day?'

4 When planning a day out or a trip, set out your expectations in advance and let your children know what *they* can expect. If they know what's in store, you'll end a lot of the tiresome questions and they can relax and enjoy – without false ideas about what might be on the cards.

5 But listen to their ideas of what makes an ideal holiday – if all of you get at least some of what you want, the holiday will work more smoothly for everyone.

What Children Learn

With pre-planning, holidays can be fun, particularly if they are structured and well organized. The best holidays work with compromise and negotiation, so that everyone has an opportunity to do what they want.

Homework

The ubiquitous battle! Homework is probably the biggest cause of family battles on a day-to-day basis and far too much importance has been invested in this after-school 'activity'. The best way to cope with a reluctance to do homework is to encourage a routine and a family schedule that allots a certain amount of time when homework – and only homework – will be done. If everyone is sitting down together working (even if younger family members are colouring or reading), you are much less likely to face a showdown. Similarly, once a routine becomes established, and your child knows that fun will follow, she'll be more likely to fall in, even if the early days of establishing routine are fraught with rebellions.

What to Do

1   It's a good idea to get homework and other necessaries out of the way before dinner, unless you eat very early. Like adults, children need time to unwind before bed and if they are struggling with or resisting homework, it's bound to have an effect on their sleep. After dinner, give them a period of time in which to choose a favourite activity; set a time limit and, if necessary, put up a star chart to ensure it is maintained. If your child is used to watching television for several hours every night and you suggest a one-hour slot instead, you'll have to use some positive encouragement to implement the changes successfully.

2   If your child regularly refuses to do her homework, offer choices: 'If we do it now, I can help you, or you can do it on your own after dinner'. 'Do you want to do it now or in 20 minutes?', 'Do you want to borrow my computer or do you want to write it out?', 'Do you want to do maths first or reading?', 'Do you want to do your homework in your bedroom or at the kitchen table?' Present it as an accepted fact that the homework *will* be done, but offer her some choices as to how, when and where.

3   It is helpful for your child to start each session of homework, studying or practising with a clearly

defined goal. In other words, to finish her French studying, master a tune on the clarinet or get that front crawl stroke smoother. If she takes a minute or two at the beginning of a study session to plan her time – 10 minutes for French, 20 for geography and 2 minutes to clear her desk – she'll know where she stands and she'll have a game plan that can reduce any potential stress. Encourage your child to make a list of what she wants to achieve beforehand. A little advance planning is great for focusing the mind. Simply writing a list of the various things to do, and the order in which they should be done, can save hours of wasted time and apathetic attempts to begin. All children respond better to a 'known' quantity. While most children will resist homework and studying (for good reason!), you can help them get down to it more quickly by encouraging them to organize a game plan. If they cross off each item as they complete it, they'll feel a sense of achievement, and can actually see an end in sight. And if they know that they'll have time for fun when it's all done, they are much more likely to get cracking. But ensure your child isn't too ambitious! Set specific targets that can be easily managed in the time available.

4   Use study breaks and rewards. Humans can only function for so long at maximum efficiency before concentration begins to wane. So, encouraging your child to take a break every so often and do something rewarding in between allows her to return to work refreshed.

5   Encourage your child to leave her desk or bedroom tidy for the next session. Most people don't bother to tidy up until the beginning of the next study session. When they finish the session, they leave everything in a mess. The problem with this is that the mess

becomes a barrier to starting the next session.
Encourage your child to spend the last minutes of the
study period getting organized for the next session.

6 Find your child's best time of day. She may have little
choice when to study, or it may not matter anyway,
but some people work better, or more easily, at
particular times of the day. Some people are morning
workers; others work best in the evenings. If your
child has preferences, try to accommodate them.

7 Encourage short study periods. Many children are
reluctant to study or to do their homework because
they believe that once they get down to it they should
keep at it for hours. This is so daunting that they
actually do nothing at all. It is much better to have
more modest goals and actually do the work. Keep
sessions short.

8 Cut big projects into slices. Big projects can be
daunting at the beginning and dispiriting in the
middle when the enthusiasm has paled. Large
projects do need to be tackled systematically. In other
words, help your child to set small, manageable tasks
that will eventually lead to tackling the large task.

9 Encourage your child to finish what she starts.

10 Reward your child for each study period. All children
enjoy doing things if they have been rewarded and
they will be more likely to want to do them again.
Have a snack between sessions and an hour doing
whatever your child finds relaxing at the end. At the
end of an exam period, you could plan a big outing or
treat that works as a carrot to learning!

11 Consider whether the demands placed upon your
child are too high. If she's expected to do simply too
much work in the evenings or in the holidays, talk to
her teacher about it. Chances are she is not alone. Ask
that homework be set for a specific period, rather

than on a task-completion basis. A friend of mine was incensed that her child had homework over the holidays, when she felt he should be resting and spending time with his family. She brought it up at a parent–teacher forum and the result? Holiday homework was abolished. Sometimes it takes just one brave individual to make the difference.

12 Make sure you aren't making the process more painful. If you demand perfection, criticize, try to teach new methods or generally show disapproval for the way your child goes about things, she's never going to want to begin a session.

13 Don't become too involved in the homework or try to do it for your child. Encourage and reward initiative and hard work, but don't overemphasize it. You don't want your child spending hours labouring over something to please you. Homework is merely an extension of what she's done all day long. Underplay it and suggest she does her best for an agreed period of time. You'll get no brownie points for doing your child's homework (although I once complained about getting an A minus for a rather marvellous bit of colouring I did for my child), and you can hamper her development. Teachers aren't stupid. They know that if work improves dramatically when it's done outside the confines of the classroom, it's not likely to be down to the individual child. Give your child a chance.

What Children Learn

That however daunting or tiresome something might be, it helps to plan it, break it into manageable chunks and then get on with it. Procrastination only drags things on and on. They learn basic time management and pride in producing work that reflects their effort. They also learn the art of concentration for periods of time, and see that hard work can always be rewarded by a little break, relaxation, fun and free time.

Maintenance

If a good routine suddenly goes out the window, work out if there is a problem at school, or if your child feels unconfident about attempting something. If there is a problem with understanding, speak to your child's teacher. Show patience and validate her worries, but show that giving things a try often breaks the backbone of the task, and things are often not as bad as she thought. Be patient with mistakes. That's how children learn. Above all, make homework an essential part of a routine, but not the be-all and end-all of your child's academic career. And remember, a few nights of no homework never hurt anyone. Break the rules from time to time to give everyone a break.

Hyperactivity

(ADD – attention deficit disorder – and ADHD – attention deficit and hyperactivity disorder)

Watch out for this diagnosis. Over the past few years it has become increasingly common to label lively and uncooperative children – some of whom do or do not have emotional or learning difficulties – as hyperactive, or suffering from ADD. The term ADD developed after several years of misnomers for children who failed to conform to what were probably idealistic standards of learning and behaviour. Such children were considered to have minimal brain disease (MBD), which later became minimal brain dysfunction when no 'disease' could be diagnosed. But it became clear that there was no dysfunction either, and with parents and practitioners demanding an explanation, the terms ADD and ADHD were developed.

In *The Limits of Biological Treatments for Psychological Distress* (S. Fisher, R. Greenberg, Lawrence Erlbaum Associates, 1989), Diane McGuinness says, 'It is currently fashionable to treat approximately one-third of all elementary school boys as an abnormal population because they are fidgety, inattentive and unamenable to adult control.' She insists that two decades of research have not provided any support for the validity of ADD and concludes that there is no convincing evidence that medications help learning or attention problems. She says that while Ritalin may 'reduce fidgety behaviour', it does so in ALL children, regardless of diagnosis. She says, 'The data consistently fails to support any benefits from stimulant medication', and cautions that stimulant medication is a drastic invasion of the body and nervous system. She also notes that the majority of children labelled as being ADD are, in fact, normal, healthy, energetic children.

ADD is not a medically diagnosed condition, meaning that it doesn't have a set list of symptoms or a fixed biological diagnosis. Children are assessed against a checklist of behaviours, which can lead to all sorts of problems. In fact, it is diagnosed when a child fits the description of 8 out of 14 items on a checklist of characteristics, and has done for six months or more. Some of these characteristics include:

- loses things necessary to complete a task
- fidgets in his seat
- can't wait his turn
- blurts out answers
- shifts from one uncompleted activity to another
- has difficulty remaining seated
- interrupts or intrudes

It doesn't take a psychologist to assess the fact that the majority of these characteristics are common to most children, particularly those in stressful conditions.

Many experts now believe that ADD has become nothing more than a buzzword. The reason that children are hyperactive or have difficulty concentrating is probably due more to the fact that:

- Western diets are so poor
- children are forced at an increasingly early age to sit still in a classroom or nursery with large numbers of other children
- they watch too much television
- they get inadequate sleep
- they get little or no exercise

Place these restrictions on any adult and the same behaviours could be expected.

Alarmingly, there are numerous studies showing that teachers believe most of their students have deficits, disorders or problems. In one study, 57 per cent of boys and 42 per cent of girls were deemed 'overactive'. In another study of boys, 30 per cent were called 'overactive', 46 per cent 'disruptive', 43 per cent had a 'short' attention span. It also appears that the vast majority of children labelled ADD are boys, which throws into question our societal expectations of children who are naturally active, aggressive and independent.

Drugs have been used as a solution to this problem, particularly Ritalin, which has the effect of temporarily calming children (all children). But this practice is now under review. For example, Sweden has abolished Ritalin as dangerous and too easily abused. *Clinical Psychiatry News* cites a Duke University study that concluded, 'the amount of trouble that children are causing adults, particularly teachers, appears to be the driving force determining children's referrals to mental health services'. In March 2000, the US government announced an effort to reverse the dramatic increase in prescriptions for psychotropic drugs such as Ritalin in pre-schoolers. In addition, the US Food and Drug Administration (FDA) is developing new labelling that addresses paediatric indications for Ritalin and other psychotropic medications, and the National Institutes of Health (NIH) in the US is conducting a nationwide study of the use of medication for attention deficit/hyperactivity disorder in children under the age of seven.

What to Do

1   Some studies show that children with a tendency towards hyperactivity benefit from increased parental attention – on a one-to-one basis. Many children are labelled 'difficult', 'hyperactive' or 'hard work' when they first exhibit these symptoms, and in some cases this can create a self-fulfilling prophecy. This type of negative labelling can harm a child emotionally, so it is important to offer positive reinforcement and to raise your child's self-respect (*see page 68*).

2   There should be a period of quality time every day, in which positive behaviour can be reinforced. Discipline should never be harsh, as your child is not usually wilfully being naughty, but simply losing control. Removing your child from the scene of a tantrum or outburst, or whatever behaviour has got out of control, will help. Time-out (*see page 79*) seems to help with some hyperactive children because it gives them the space to calm down, without unnecessary stimulation.

3   Some children naturally have increased energy and physical requirements. It is important for any child

with these tendencies to get plenty of exercise. This can mean a break not offered to other children in a school environment. Talk to your child's teacher about allowing more breaks for physical release of tension (running around the playground, for example), which will help children to focus more in the classroom.

4   If your child is extremely active, you may want to consider whether early schooling is a good idea. Many children are not able to handle the confines of a school environment until they are older, and it can exacerbate a problem if you start too early. It is, of course, very difficult for parents to deal with a constantly active child, and you will need to get as much support and help as you can from friends, family and professionals.

5   Make your daily routine as simple and straightforward as possible. It will help to keep your child calmer and he will have more chance of remembering what comes next. Try to avoid rushing around or eating on the hop, which will make him feel unsettled.

6   Be very specific when talking to your child. Explain everything, and don't expect too much.

7   Avoid over-stimulation. Playtime should be calm and reassuring, and no more than one or two other playmates should be involved. When things get out of hand, change the room or the venue (head off to the park, for example).

8   Remember that hyperactivity is not bad behaviour. There can be learning difficulties present, and your child may have some difficulty with coordination or controlling movement.

9   Dietary causes are now credibly linked with diagnoses of ADD and ADHD. Food allergy, toxic overload and nutritional deficiencies can be at the root of the

problem. It may help to see a nutritionist to ensure your child's diet is contributing towards an even temperament and energy levels.

What Children Learn

Even the most energetic or hyperactive child needs to feel he is accepted and loved. If you can build his self-respect, he will shrug off the inevitable labels that come his way and learn to believe in himself. Most cases of hyperactivity are confined to childhood and outgrown. Remember that your child will need to feel 'normal' and be able to solve problems, make decisions, take responsibility, interact with others, learn to negotiate and sustain relationships, and develop self-esteem and self-liking. If your child is given every chance to do these things, he will learn that he is as capable, bright and likeable as everyone else.

Maintenance

With a hyperactive child, things can go awry quite easily, so it's important to stick to a tightly constructed routine as much as possible. You may need the patience of a saint at times, so ensure you have regular breaks for self-nurturing. If you can go away and come back refreshed, you'll find it a lot easier to cope. Try to keep an eye on diet, which can cause behaviour problems and may be at the root of many setbacks. Above all, help your child to feel good about himself and he'll know he has the power to learn to control and channel his behaviour into more positive activities.

Illness

Having an ill child can turn the household on its head. Routines go out the window; your concern can feed the tension in other children and test the relationship; the ill child gets used to being pampered and given a lot of TLC, so that she can, in some cases, grow to expect it; and you may find that your patience wears impossibly thin. What's more, when children see that illness gains them all sorts of treats and attention, they are more likely to feign it when they feel they need more from you. Some children also use illness as an excuse to avoid things they don't want to do. The latter two cases are something that needs to be avoided at all cost.

What to Do

1   Remember that stress and emotional problems in children often manifest themselves as physical symptoms. When they don't feel well, even emotionally, they often choose something they know will mean something to you: a tummy ache, an earache, a headache, sore throat. What they really feel is hard for them to verbalize, so they latch on to something that expresses the fact that they don't feel themselves. Help them to work out whether it is a genuine illness or if their emotions are at the root. Encourage them to express their feelings in order to get help, rather than saying 'I feel sick'.

2   If your child says she doesn't feel well, take her seriously instead of assuming the worst. With a little TLC, she may feel stronger emotionally to deal with whatever is troubling her.

3   If you think she's avoiding school or another activity by pretending to be ill, ask some leading questions and show understanding: 'I wonder if there might be something happening at school – you don't seem yourself at the moment,' for example.

4   Don't dismiss the idea of a day off for your child to recharge her batteries. Periods of low emotional health are often a precursor to physical illness and if she can rest, relax and have a little time on her own,

you may nip the problem in the bud. This doesn't advocate skiving; it is a realistic tool for your child to use in order to evaluate her own wellbeing and take steps towards feeling better. No one benefits (adults and children alike) from driving themselves into the ground. All of us need to learn when the warning bells are ringing, and to stop and take a break.

5   Don't go overboard with a genuinely ill child. If you pamper them too much, they'll learn to use illness as a tool for gaining your attention. They may also develop unhealthy ideas about illness and what is required. A robust approach, with lots of care and TLC as well as a positive viewpoint ('I'm sure you'll be up and about tomorrow'), will help your child see illness as a temporarily inconvenient situation.

What Children Learn

Children learn to listen to their bodies and work out when they are ill – when they need an emotional health 'break', for example, and when what they feel is not illness at all, but an emotion that needs sorting. They see that expressing themselves and asking for help when they have problems is much more effective than playing ill, which will, in the end, become a little like crying wolf.

Maintenance

If your child regularly and inexplicably becomes ill, it's time to open the communication channels and find out what is at the root of the problem. Give her space to relax and take the odd day off if she feels she really needs it. It's a lesson that most adults could learn. Don't be too harsh on a child who is 'faking'. She clearly has a reason for it. Simply point out that you aren't sure she really is ill, so maybe you could work out together what else could be making her feel unwell.

Interrupting

If there is one thing that drives most parents crazy, it's interruptions. Most parents feel that they devote much of their days to their children. When they finally have a moment to chat on the telephone or take a little time to do something without the children (reading a book or the paper, watching television, chatting with a partner), they are constantly thwarted. The main problem is that children tend to see parents as their own 'possession', and feel threatened when your attention is elsewhere. And being intrinsically selfish creatures, children also tend to see your time and activities as far less important than their own.

What to Do

1   Teach a little respect. Make it clear that when you are on the telephone or doing something without them, you do not expect to be interrupted. There are always times when an interruption might be necessary – something extremely important to be imparted or a genuine emergency – but in these cases children need to learn to break into your time/conversation/space with respect. 'Excuse me' is a good start or 'Sorry to interrupt' or even 'I can see you are busy'.

2   Practise the same respect for your children. If they are busy doing something, don't barge in and feel you have the right to their attention. Use the same phrases. You are much more likely to teach this type of behaviour by example than by shouting when they interrupt yet again.

3   For younger children, pre-plan. Explain that you are going to be on the telephone, or doing whatever, and say that you will be busy until you tell them you are not. Give them a book or a toy and set them up

nearby, so they don't feel they have completely lost you. If they interrupt, ignore them or shake your head. They will soon learn that you mean business.

4   Explain in advance what you are doing and how much time you need. 'I have a friend coming round', for example, 'and I will be talking to her for about a half an hour. I expect no interruptions. I'll let you know when I am ready.'

5   Make sure you use this technique for time with your kids, too, so that they feel equally special. Advise siblings that you will be spending time with one child and do not expect interruptions. Do it for all of them.

What Children Learn

Respect for you and your time. They also learn that they are loved and important, and worthy of your respect as well. They will see that being with other people or focusing on other things does not negate their feelings for you. It simply means taking time for yourself.

Maintenance

If interruptions continue to be a problem, bring up the issue at a family meeting and work out strategies for your children to keep themselves occupied while you are doing other things. Make them proud of the fact that they can keep themselves busy. Reward attempts to leave you some peace. The behaviour will soon become learned.

Jealousy

This is a natural emotion for all human beings, no matter how hard we try to deny it. Your children may be jealous of friends, their possessions, their achievements. They are even more likely to be jealous of siblings, who always, in a child's eyes, seem to be getting a better deal. Underpinning

most jealousy is dissatisfaction or the misguided belief
that they are not as good as someone else.

What to Do

1   Remember that you can never be completely equal
    with children, nor should you try. What children
    really need is for their perceived needs to be met. In
    other words, you need to find out what each child
    really feels he needs and wants, and then take steps
    towards ensuring that at least some of those needs
    and desires are met. One child may think he doesn't
    get as much attention as a sibling, in which case
    attention is his perceived requirement. Another child
    may feel he doesn't get equal freedom, which is an
    issue you can sit down and work out together. Take
    the time to find out what your child really cares about
    and you'll be halfway to solving the problem.

2   Let your children know that possessions and
    achievements are not likely to get them more
    attention from their friends, peers or parents. What
    makes them special and likeable and important is
    them. Their unique characteristics. Work on building
    your child's self-respect (*see page 68*), so that he feels
    valuable in his own right. Children who feel good
    about themselves have much less need to envy others
    because they feel content.

3   Keep open the lines of communication so you can
    work out areas where your child feels dissatisfied,
    undervalued or threatened. In these situations, he'll
    want something that someone else has in the
    misguided view that it will be the magic wand to
    rectify all problems. Teach your child to be realistic
    (*see page 187*). Having it all often means having
    nothing because you don't value or appreciate things.
    Give him responsibility; teach him the value of

money; focus on the important things in life that are right on his doorstep. Let him see that having a loving family, freedom, support, affection, fun and unconditional love are ideals to which many, many people aspire, and point out that there are probably an awful lot of people who are jealous of *him*!

What Children Learn

That jealousy is a negative emotion that festers, and that it is much better to express their needs and to work towards having the important ones met. They will also see that the things they envy are not always things that make people happy. You could give in and buy him that bike, but would it really change the feelings of inadequacy that are underpinning his intense need for it?

Maintenance

Remember that jealous feelings will spring up from time to time. Teach your child that there is no shame in admitting being jealous, and help him work out why something matters so much to him. Satisfy perceived needs, find replacements, but above all, teach your child to accept that happiness can be found in other ways.

Listening

One of the most frustrating aspects of parenting is trying to get a message across to – or open a conversation with – a child who simply refuses to listen. Some children pretend to listen while their thoughts are elsewhere; others ignore you; and some little monkeys even go as far as to hold their hands over their ears or walk away. Given that communication is the most crucial tool in the discipline game, it's enormously distressing when you can't get your child to hear what you are saying.

What to Do

1   One of the problems might be that you talk too much.
Sounds harsh, but if you are constantly lecturing,
cajoling, reminding, nagging, advising or simply just
chattering, your child is going to tune out. Even the
brightest children may find it hard to decipher the
important stuff from the slosh in between. Leave your
child to her own resources. Chat, definitely, but if you
really want her to listen, you'll have to stop the verbal
diarrhoea.

2   Show that you have the ability to listen too, and
really hear what your child is saying (*see page 3*).
This promotes mutual respect.

3   Make sure that all conversations with your child
aren't geared to bad behaviour or 'heavy' subjects.
Take the opportunity to sit down and say you just
wanted to point out some positive things you've
noticed. If she learns that you aren't always nagging,
and that you do have interesting and rewarding things
to impart, she is more likely to listen.

4   Keep your voice down – whisper, even. Children tend
to be excited when things sound secretive and fun.
Use this technique to break a cycle of child deafness.

5   Occasionally ask them to repeat what you just said.
You'll catch them off guard. If they can't repeat it, say
something tantalizing like: 'I guess you won't find out
what was in it for you' and leave it. They might pay a
bit more attention in future.

6   If your toddler refuses to listen, pare down the words
to basic messages. Or stop talking altogether (unless
there is a safety issue). Continue to look her in the
eye. Smile and show affection, but let her realize that
it is far better having a speaking parent than one who
is noticeably silent.

7 Ask your child if she has a moment (showing respect) to listen to something important. If she says she doesn't, ask her to choose a convenient time. She cannot, then, claim that you caught her unawares, or that she is 'busy'.

8 Don't say things you don't mean, whether they are threats or promises. Your child will soon learn that your words are often empty, and stop listening.

9 Keep things simple. Complicated instructions may be too difficult to follow and your child will lose interest.

10 Speak to your child with respect, and take the time to listen yourself. When you have her attention, keep it short and sweet. Ask for her opinions and involve her in the conversation. Speak as you would to an adult, in a level voice and making things interesting. No child will ever respond to baby talk or being talked down to, nor will she tolerate being talked at. A conversation takes more than one, and if you expect to get anything back – or for anything to go in – you need to involve her and stimulate her curiosity and interest.

What Children Learn

That listening doesn't mean one more tirade of things they have done wrong; that it can lead to productive sessions where their views are taken into consideration, their feelings validated and their accomplishments and efforts noticed and rewarded. They can learn to respect you and what you have to say, particularly if you show them the same respect by listening back.

Maintenance

Keep up the communication and make it easy and comfortable. Ensure that your child feels that a 'talk' doesn't mean trouble, and that most of what you have to say is positive and productive. Show respect and behave as you'd like your children to behave. Do you really listen to them? When you stop listening, everything slips.

Lying

Children lie for various reasons. I rather doubt any of us can hold up our hands and say we've never told one. Often, children lie to protect their parents' feelings or to make them feel better. More often, however, it is because they fear recrimination, punishment or rejection, and they feel cornered into a situation where their only choice is to get out fast, with a little lie. Chronic liars may do so because they lack self-respect and believe that inventing things will make them more exciting, interesting, fun to be with, or somehow a better person. All parents need to understand the motivation behind their children's lies before they can work out the solution. There's no point in saying that lying is 'wrong'. They've probably seen you do it on one occasion or another (white lies, of course) and you'll be sending confusing messages.

What to Do

1   Without causing them to lose face, point out when you know they aren't telling the truth. Something along the lines of: 'Good try. I wish I was as imaginative as you are. You should be a writer. Now, how about what really happened.' Show humour, and let your child know that you aren't going to punish him.

2   Don't corner your child with questions that invite lies: 'Did you come straight home from school?' (when you know he didn't) is going to make him feel trapped. Say something like: 'I suspect you didn't

come right home from school. Did something happen on the way home?'

3   Ensure your child is able to take pride in himself and his accomplishments. If he feels good about himself, has self-esteem and knows he is valued and loved for who he is, he's much less likely to reinvent himself and his life by lying.

4   Respect privacy. Sometimes there are things your children may not want to talk about, or share. Allow them this space. Pushing them to share things they do not consider your business or relevant to you is inviting dishonesty.

5   Try not to be too judgmental or hard on your children when they do confide in you. If they learn that they get nowhere with honesty, they might as well go down the less honest route.

6   Let your children know that it is acceptable – and normal – to make mistakes. Covering them up doesn't help anyone. Mistakes can be used to learn something from a situation. Help your child to uncover what that might be.

7   Make sure your child feels loved – no matter what he does. Many children lie to spare their parents' feelings or to prevent them from being disappointed.

What Children Learn

That it is always a good idea to tell the truth and it prevents the tangled web of deceit that lies often create. They learn that people forgive a lot easier if they are presented with the truth, and that lying is disrespectful and insulting. They also see that it is OK to make mistakes, and that they have the support and love of their families to help them find solutions.

Maintenance

Try not to over-control your child or he will feel threatened and pressured and likely to make himself and his activities out to be rosier than they really are. Continue to encourage regular communication – of both the good and bad things in your child's life – and avoid being judgmental. Show appreciation that your child is being honest, even if you don't always agree with an action he has taken. Look for self-respect issues if the problem persists, and take steps to ensure that your child feels valuable in his own right.

Manners

Left to their own resources, most children have the table manners of cavemen. Without the watchful eye of an adult, it's hard to believe that the majority of them have been taught any manners at all. Does it matter? Manners, like social skills, are important in most circumstances. But once learned, they can usually be dragged out and dusted off when appropriate, and as long as your child knows when to use them and why, you are in with a chance. If you have high expectations and take manners very seriously, you'll need to make your expectations known early on and keep drumming it in. Kids might learn by rote and behave appropriately in your company, but given the opportunity, they'll relax and do what they please. The bottom line is, really, that manners are a personal issue, and you have to work out what is acceptable to you and your family.

What to Do

1   Work on the important things: being polite, saying
    please and thank you, and answering questions when

asked. If you have no problems with this, you can move on to the tougher things, like looking a person in the eye when you are talking to them, returning a greeting or an enquiry about how well you are with something similar, shaking hands and maintaining polite conversation. If you are really pernickety, you can encourage your sons to open doors for women, give up their seats on the bus or train and pull out their chair when they sit down. All of these behaviours can be learned.

2   But work out what is important to you. If you nit-pick you are going to meet with some resistance and possibly some rebellion. Remember that all children develop social skills at different ages, and yours will undoubtedly adopt them when it is absolutely necessary. In fact, you may find that in important situations, your boorish son becomes positively princely. Give them the messages, explain why it's important (respect, courtesy, politeness, etc.), reinforce them from time to time, and you'll find that they will use them when required.

3   Request and expect basic table manners and politeness at home (of the 'excuse me' variety), but let your child let her hair down a little in her own environment. Chances are that you do things at home you wouldn't do in public. As long as your child knows the difference between public and private behaviour, she'll be fine.

4   Make teaching manners a game. Quiz them: 'What do you say if someone says "how do you do?"'; 'Which fork do you use for your starter?'; 'What are napkins for?' (expect some imaginative ideas for this one); 'What do you say when someone gives you a gift?'; 'What do you do if you don't like it?' (pretend you do, of course). Kids love quizzes, and they'll learn the

lessons without you having to nag. You could pretend, for an evening, that you are the Royal Family. Exaggerate everything and make a joke of it. It's a good way to work out how much your kids have really taken in!

5   Give your child a knife and fork from day one, even if they don't use them. They'll learn what to do by seeing others and work out the connection between the cutlery on their tray. Very small children who are being weaned can be given soft plastic or acrylic cutlery with which to experiment. Offer cutlery appropriate to age.

6   Be polite yourself. Say please and thank you to your children. Excuse yourself from the table. Thank someone for a lovely meal. Ask politely to interrupt a conversation. Children will learn much more from this approach than they ever will from being nagged.

What Children Learn

They learn appropriate behaviour for different situations, and they can hold their own, whatever company they end up keeping. They also learn that courtesy is the hallmark of respect, and when they treat people politely, they get a very positive response.

Maintenance

At various stages it becomes 'cool' to be slovenly, surly and completely bereft of manners. Treat this as a stage of life, rather than a disaster, and continue to behave politely yourself. If you draw attention to it, you'll make it into a bigger issue than it needs to be and probably feed a little rebellious behaviour. Let it blow over. If your children categorically refuse to show any sign of manners, it may be that you are putting too much emphasis on it, and they have decided that it's a great way to get your attention. Cool off and let them see they aren't going to wind you up. They'll eventually decide that it's easier to model positive behaviour and get your praise than it is to try to make you annoyed.

Masturbation

Most children explore their bodies as a part of development. The last thing you want to do is make them feel their bodies are something to be ashamed of, or that getting pleasure from touching themselves (something that links inevitably to their feelings about sex later in life) is somehow wrong. If you have religious views on the subject, try to avoid shaming your child or making him feel guilty or frightened about doing something that feels nice. You may find that you increase the fascination (through a little rebellion) or that you unwittingly affect his later sexuality.

What to Do

1   The best thing to do is ignore it. It's a private pursuit and it really isn't any of your business. What you do need to get across is that it is not normally socially acceptable for people to touch their genitals in public. Gently point this out and suggest that it is better saved for the privacy of the bedroom.

2   Very young children naturally play with their genitals and this can be completely ignored. If you focus on it, they are likely to become even more fascinated.

3   If there seems to be an inordinate amount of time spent masturbating, you might want to ensure that your children have enough activities and interests in their lives. It may well be that they are simply bored and they while away the hours doing something that causes pleasure.

4   Show some respect. Don't check up on teenage boys who spend a lot of time in their bedrooms alone, or in the bathroom. Give them some space.

What Children Learn

That they are in charge of their bodies and the feelings that are produced. That sexuality is personal and can be explored in private. That their bodies or their activities are never considered 'dirty' or 'wrong', but normal and acceptable.

Maintenance

If you have a real problem with masturbation, there may be issues that need professional help. And by a real problem, I mean something that is affecting their lifestyle.

Materialism and the Kiddie Consumer Culture

Whether it's clothes, computers, games consoles, CDs or sports equipment, increased materialism affects our children both now and in the future. First of all, they develop a need for and interest in material goods, which they will begin to associate with affection and love. This focus can become obsessive. Children will require more and more to satisfy them, and to reassure themselves that they are important and loved. Second, it creates an instant-gratification scenario, in which children demand and receive. They do not learn the art of patience, of financial management, of working hard for something (which imbues a sense of achievement) and of caring for things. If things are quickly and easily replaced, they lose interest and are on to the next 'big' thing. It throws them into the big 'competition' ring with their friends, where they feel inadequate and upset when they do not have everything that their friends have.

It's a difficult scenario. Children are fed this type of attitude by the media, which create reasons why their products are essential, must-have items. And when their peers (*see page 51*) are perceived to have more or better gear, they become obsessed.

What to Do

1   Be honest with your children about the things you believe are important. If you balk at spending £100 on a pair of football boots, don't. Explain that you don't feel comfortable spending that kind of money on something you feel he doesn't need. But give him choices. Tell him that the maximum sum in mind was £50. You are willing to buy him a pair for that amount, or contribute that sum to a more expensive pair. If he wants something that badly, he might be

prepared to work to make up the difference. If he won't, it can't be that important.

2 When you are shopping, or they are making a Christmas list, for example, make it clear the number of items you are prepared to buy. For older children, explain the limits of your budget. It's amazing how well children respond to this approach. They may take hours or days choosing, but they will come up with things that meet your criteria.

3 Teach your children the difference between *wanting* and *needing*. Show willing to provide for needs, and then negotiate the wants. Ask them to explain to you why they need something. If they can come up with a reasonable, rational and well-thought-out set of reasons, you may want to reconsider.

4 Teach children to budget. From an early age, they can be given (or earn) pocket money, which goes for 'extras'. Don't be tempted to top it up, except on special occasions. They'll learn that if they really want something, they'll need to save, budget or plan. If you give in, they'll learn to expect it.

5 Ensure that children are grateful for what they get. Expect a thank you, and thank them and others when you are given things. Don't encourage children to rip into presents at Christmas or birthdays without giving due consideration to each gift. All children need to learn appreciation, and to consider the thought that went into the choice of gift.

6 If your child makes a mistake and spends his money on something that proved disappointing or useless, commiserate, but help him see what lessons he might have learned from poor decision-making. Ultimately, all children need to learn the value of money and the importance of making the right choices. Mistakes are part of the process.

What Children Learn

The skills of money-management, decision-making, saving and defining the difference between needs and wants. They also learn the value of money, and see that everything in life needs to be worked for. Above all, however, they will learn that love does not mean getting material goods from others. Give them everything they want, and that's exactly the assumption they will make.

Maintenance

Watch your own lifestyle. If you are materialistic, you will instil these qualities in your children. Don't be afraid to live simply, with occasional treats within your budget. Consider why you might be overindulging your child. Do you feel guilty that you aren't around as much as you should be? Help your child to see that resources – even in wealthy families, whose outgoings tend to swell to meet their income – are necessarily limited and that choices will always have to be made. Continue to show faith in his ability to manage his own money and to make decisions.

Motivation, Lack of

This problem is similar to apathy (*see page 100*), but it differs slightly. Children who lack motivation may not be apathetic. They may simply not see why something is worth doing, or they may not feel inspired to try. Problems with motivation are often reflected in schoolwork, a refusal to help around the house or to become involved with the family, or to try their best in a given situation.

The reasons for this are multifold. Some children may not try because they know it drives you crazy. It's a bit like saying 'you can't make me' and, indeed, you may find that you can't. The result? A power struggle in which no one is prepared to budge. Your child may be afraid of failure and therefore will not even begin to try new things. She may be under pressure and feel that she cannot live up to expectations. She may doubt herself and feel that it is easier to avoid challenging situations – or indeed anything that challenges her – in order to maintain a bit of peace.

What to Do

1   This is a frustrating problem for parents because, ultimately, you cannot invest a child with enthusiasm if she doesn't feel it. Don't be tempted to bully or push your child harder, or even make her feel silly or useless for being the way she is. That will only serve to destroy the communication between you, as well as the mutual respect.

2   Show respect for her situation, and love and understanding for the way she is feeling. If she doesn't feel 'bad' or that she is letting you down, she'll be able to let go of some of her negative feelings that might be driving the behaviour.

3   Ensure that the attention you give her is not focused on achievements or tasks. If you only ever spend time with your kids over dinner or homework – both situations that tend to involve some nagging and the presentation of your expectations – she's likely to pull back and opt out altogether. Spend some time doing fun, uncompetitive, relaxing things: a walk in the park, a game, listening to music, or just chatting about nothing in particular.

4   Analyse your expectations. If you expect your child to be perfect or the best, she may realize she'll never achieve what you expect, and opt out of trying. She may be more aware of her capabilities than you are! You need to encourage your child to be *her* best – the

best *she* can be. Effort is more important than achievement.

5   Set small goals that you know are achievable, and make a fuss of her successes. Every time she gets one under her belt, she'll be more confident about carrying on.

6   Keep up the communication. Talk to your child about different situations and how they make her feel. Show her you are there to help her solve problems. Say that you have noticed she has lost interest in trying at school, or that she doesn't seem to care about her responsibilities in the house. Ask her how she sees things, and *listen* to her response. Maybe she feels there is too much for her to take on; whatever the reason, don't judge. Focus on solutions rather than laying blame.

7   Show plenty of encouragement. Use star charts and rewards to inspire your child to try new things and to give her best. She may have felt in the past that her efforts have gone unrecognized, making her feel 'what's the point?' If you show interest, enthusiasm and support, she'll be a lot more likely to want to be and stay involved in her pursuits.

What Children Learn

That there are always periods when we feel less inclined to give our best, but that we can pull ourselves out of this situation and get back into routine and real life. What needs to happen is a fresh start, setting some goals and working towards a reward or feeling of achievement. They'll see that they are good enough in your book, whether or not they are the best, and that you respect the effort they make. They'll also see that success is personal and effort-related. Only they can make a success of their lives, and they need to believe in themselves in order to do that.

Maintenance

During stressful periods (at school, in the playground, in times of divorce or other problems at home) many children will naturally pull back. Fear (*see page 148*) and uncertainty have an uncanny ability to pull the rug from under our children's feet, and they will need lots of love and support to get back on track. Continue to show faith and belief in your child. Recognize that she is going through a difficult period (and help her to explain why), but be positive about the future and help her realize her potential by giving her the opportunity to experience small successes along the way.

Moving

We live in a transient society. Job instability, the search for a 'better life' and other factors all mean that the average child will move home at least once before the age of 10. It's a disruptive experience for the whole family, but children can find it even more traumatic, particularly since they are virtually powerless to do anything about it.

If you are the type of person who thrives on change, you may need to curb your instincts if you have small children. All children thrive on familiarity and routine. If you constantly seek change, their social development can be hampered (usually only in the short term, but a stressful experience nonetheless). Consider the benefits of a move before you put it into action and make sure you consider your children carefully. If your child has suffered a recent trauma, such as the death of a loved one or a divorce, you may want to hold off moving until things settle a little. Many people move quickly following marital break-up, often because finances dictate such action.

However, this can intensify the problems and stress for young children. Wait as long as you can, if possible.

What to Do

1 The most important thing you can do is exhibit positive behaviour. If it's not a move you particularly want to make, try not to let your negative feelings influence your child's approach. While it's perfectly acceptable to commiserate with a child, try to point out the positive elements of the move, and actively find things that will cause your child to look forward to the change.

2 Talk about things well in advance so that your child is well and truly prepared. It might seem overly pedantic, but if he knows what to expect in every situation, he'll feel prepared and find it easier to cope. For example, discuss the location of the nearest park, the nice new school, the other children you saw playing, the social clubs, the big new bedroom and the ease of communication with friends left behind.

3 Your child may sense that you are not 100 per cent happy with the move and be keeping mum to avoid further upset. Remember that all children will find a change difficult, and you need to draw out, face and find ways to discuss and cope with his fears and concerns.

4 Involve your child in the decision-making process as much as possible. If redecorating is on the cards, ask him to choose his own room colour or a new piece of furniture. If you are choosing between two houses, ask for and listen to his opinion. Remember, he has to live there too!

5 Don't look upon a move as a perfect opportunity for a mass clear-out. Your child will want to see lots of his old familiar belongings around, even those he

cherished as a small child and no longer looks at. These are links to his past and are important, if only in the short term, for a successful move.

6   If your child is at school, try to move in the summer, or at a stage where he would be changing schools anyhow. No child wants to feel different or be the 'new kid on the block', so make the change when there is the least possible disruption.

7   Try to arrange play sessions, or get-togethers, before school starts, so that your child knows at least one or two familiar faces.

8   Teenagers are another kettle of fish altogether, and you may find that scenes and rebellions become the family norm for some time. Remember that it's often difficult to establish a trusted group of peers, and the prospect of starting all over can be very daunting for an adolescent. Take note of his feelings and suggest that a girlfriend or boyfriend, or a few of his old mates, can come to stay from time to time. Don't discount the importance of adolescent relationships. Show empathy and respect for his concerns, and do as much as you can to ease the transition.

9   Have realistic expectations for your child. Teachers generally expect an adjustment period of about six weeks. Some children may take less time; some may need more. Your child will need your continuing support.

Naps

By the age of three or four, most children outgrow the need for naps. But before that, they can be a godsend. Paradoxically, regular naps will help encourage good night-time sleep habits by ensuring that your child doesn't become overtired and unable to settle, and by making falling asleep a routine part of life. Your baby or child will be much less likely to accept bedtime, and missing household activity, if she is unused to taking naps. Furthermore, babies and young children do need a great deal of sleep and it is unlikely they will get enough in the night-time hours alone. Regular sleep establishes a good sleep-wake cycle that will ensure their needs are met.

But as good as it may be for them, you can expect some resistance. It's daylight, everyone else is having fun, and your child has been excluded, confined to a cot or bed with nothing to do but *sleep*.

What to Do

1   Make naps a part of your routine from the very earliest days. If you haven't managed to swing it, it's never too late to start. Ensure that the lead-up is pleasurable, beginning with a story, for example, or a snuggle in the rocking chair, or a little chat together in the bedroom. Then put your baby or child to bed, kiss her and close the door.

2   Use the same techniques for problems going to bed (*see page 105*).

3   If she doesn't fall asleep naturally, read her a story or give her a book to look at. Put on a story tape or some gentle music. Make sure she knows that you mean business! If you allow her to climb out of bed and join in the activities in other parts of the house, you'll never instil good sleeping habits.

4   For a few days, your child or baby might cry or whine or demand attention. Reassure her that you are there, but don't let her get up. She may just play for a while and doze off, or she may draw on her considerable resources to force herself to stay awake. Don't give up. Continue to put her down at the same time every day. Eventually she'll get the message that she might

as well sleep. But even if she only rests in the comfort of her bedroom, she'll come out refreshed and ready for action.

5   To help your baby fall asleep at a reasonable hour, don't let her nap past 3 or 4pm. At least four hours should elapse between the end of an afternoon nap and bedtime.

What Children Learn

To fall asleep on their own, and to enjoy rest as a part of a comforting routine. They learn that although you will always be there, they aren't going to win a battle by shouting, crying or screaming.

Maintenance

Stick to the routine and it should become just that – routine. There are times, however, when things fly out the window: when your child is sick, for example, or when she outgrows the need for a nap. She may also be angry at you for something and refuse to be put down. Remain firm, loving, affectionate and show genuine interest in their feelings. But remind yourself that nap time also offers you a little space to get on with other things. It's as good for you to develop this routine as it is for your child. Continue to encourage a 'rest-time' for a few weeks after it is clear that she no longer needs to sleep during the day. All children need to learn to take some time out to recharge their batteries. Play a story tape; give her a choice of toy animal to take into bed to cuddle; make her feel she has some power over the situation, but that it is going to happen.

New Baby

There is nothing better to stir up the family dynamic and routine than a new baby. Although your other children may love the idea, the reality may be somewhat different. Expect feelings of jealousy and envy, frustration that they no longer have your full attention whenever they want it, concern that their position in the family has been usurped, and even feelings of being unloved or no longer important.

What to Do

1   Remember that new babies don't need a great deal more than feeding, nappy changing, bathing and sleeping for the first little while. As long as you are there when required, they will be content and happy. The person or people that need you most are your other children. Focus on them. Don't talk too much about the new baby; show an interest in what they are up to. Try to keep things as routine as possible.

2   Don't fall into the trap of making your other children little helpers. They might like the responsibility from time to time, but they will end up resenting the baby for taking up so much of their time.

3   Do get them involved in things they might find pleasurable, and praise them for their efforts. Point out how much the baby likes them, and how they are so 'good' with him or her. Show pride in any effort they make or any interest they show.

4   Talk about how things were when your other children were babies – laugh at the funny things they might have done. Share some moments when you particularly enjoyed holding them or cuddling them. Show them that they had the same love and affection that you are now giving your baby and that you treasure the memories. All children love talking about themselves; give them the opportunity.

5   Don't make a fuss about a new baby in front of his or her siblings. They will think they are right in the belief that they have been replaced.

6   Let your child express how he feels, and help him
    with the words: 'You must be feeling a bit jealous that
    the baby is getting all these presents', or 'It must be
    frustrating that we can't go out to the park in the
    afternoon because the baby is sleeping.' If he knows
    his feelings are normal and that you sympathize with
    his position, he'll feel mollified.

What Children Learn

That you have enough love to go around and that their
position in the family will never be threatened, no matter
how many intruders arrive on the scene. They'll see that
they can take some pleasure from a new member of the
family, and take some pride in sharing the responsibility of
keeping the baby happy. That routines may change, but
you will always be there when they need you.

Maintenance

At different stages of your new baby's life, he or she will
undoubtedly demand – and get – more of your attention.
Try to explain in advance what is happening and why. Say
that you also feel a bit cheated that you don't have quite as
much time to play and talk. Try and take some extra time,
when the baby has gone to bed, to spend with your other
children. Let them know in advance when this will be and
do your utmost to ensure it happens. Explain the
development of your baby so that they can show some
understanding. If the baby screams and screams and
disrupts the entire household, it's not likely to incite much
sympathy. If you explain, however, that he or she is
teething, and how painful it must be, you might get a
better reaction. Above all, continue to show your children
unconditional love, and respect their achievements and
milestones as much as you do your baby's.

Night-time Waking

In a society where we are all preoccupied with sleep, and never feel that we get enough, a disrupted night's sleep can be unbearable. The problem is, of course, that most children don't share our concern. For various reasons, including stress, a disrupted sleep pattern, nightmares, illness and sometimes even a poor diet, your child may wake in the night and expect to be entertained.

What to Do

1 Remain firm. Go to your child's room. Tuck her in, speak in a low voice and gently encourage her to go back to sleep. Don't turn on the light or show anger, which will exacerbate the situation.

2 If she continues, repeat the visit two or three times, but show no interest in anything other than saying good night. If it continues, I suggest you leave your child on her own, as difficult as it may seem. If she knows she has you hopping up and out of bed every time she calls, she'll learn nothing other than power. And she's likely to want more.

3 Before bedtime, offer rewards if she can manage to stay in bed all night long. Put the star chart above her bed so she will remember. Reward her first thing in the morning for a job well done. Young children cannot wait a long time for rewards or they'll forget what they are for.

4 Remember that you give your child all the love, attention and nurturing she needs during the day. Night-time is for sleeping and you'll do her no favours if you disabuse this notion and give in. No child will be traumatized by the odd crying session, particularly if she learns that she survived the night and that things are just as happy as they ever were the next day.

5   It is a good idea to include time for a chat in your
    night-time routine, when you can draw out any
    concerns. Many children can be encouraged to talk
    when they are relaxed and away from the distractions
    of toys, homework, television or siblings. Remember
    never to be judgmental. Just listen and offer solutions
    wherever possible.

6   If your child wakes in the night with terrors, don't try
    to 'talk things through'. Just reassure your child and
    talk about it in the morning. If you are anxious, angry
    or frightened yourself, you will pass on your feelings
    to your child, which can make things worse.

7   Last of all, avoid anything that can cause anxiety in
    your child before bedtime – arguments, scary stories
    or tapes, frightening television shows or games (such
    as murder in the dark and even hide and seek).

What Children Learn

They learn to be capable and self-reliant, to get themselves
off to sleep. They also learn that there are limits to your
time and energy, and that they cannot always have what
they want, when they want it. No child ever benefits from
being allowed to manipulate her parents. She'll see that
you respect her feelings, but that you are not prepared to
budge on the rules.

Maintenance

Anything can cause your child's sleep patterns to be
disrupted. Stay firm. Stick to your guns. Show respect for
her feelings and unconditional love, but make it clear that
night-time is for sleeping and you intend to do just that in
your own bed.

No Communication

Communication is crucial both to any successful discipline plan and *every* healthy relationship. If you can't talk, you can't get to the bottom of things; you don't have the ability to problem-solve; and you can't ever have the understanding that is crucial to a positive relationship. That may all sound very negative, but if there is one thing you need to do as a parent, it is to encourage and maintain good relations.

All children go through periods of failing to communicate and there are too many reasons for this to list. They may be angry at you for something; they may feel that any communication they do have with you centres on lectures or telling them what they are doing wrong; they may simply have a lot on their plate and feel they need a little space to deal with it. Equally, however, they may feel guilty or upset about something, and worried that they will disappoint you if they spill the beans. Some children may also see that a good way to get your attention is to close down. There you'll be pestering them, fussing over them and trying too hard to talk.

What to Do

1   Good communication cannot be forced. It builds over time and its foundation is trust. Your child needs to know that he can say or express anything to you without fear of recrimination or disappointing you. Even if you are shocked or angry about something your child tells you, it's important to remain unjudgmental, to try to see things from your child's point of view and to show unconditional love and understanding. Only then will you have the tools you need to encourage a change in behaviour.

2   Ensure that your conversations are not all about discipline, schoolwork or expectations. Have some fun. Try to find some shared interests. Show some interest in *his world*. Read up on his favourite football team, read the same book as your child, watch a television programme together, tell him stories about your life and your friends. Tell jokes. Express your feelings. If conversations are unthreatening, your child is a lot more likely to engage.

3   Make sure you listen (*see page 3*). Communication simply can't exist without mutual listening *and* interaction.

4   Work out the times when your child simply needs a sounding board and some sympathy, and when he does actually want your support and help with his problems. Sometimes children just want to air a problem to get it off their chest. Let them. You don't need to be Mr or Mrs Fix-it all the time.

5   Set up times when you are alone with your child, and just see what happens. Chat about things without pressure, and don't make him feel that he has to talk. If he joins in, don't show surprise or leap in with serious questions. Just let things flow. He will talk when he is ready.

6   Don't go on and on and on when you are together. Sometimes the shortest messages are the most effective. They can spark a conversation, or they can be taken on board. If you complicate things, he's likely to tune out. Let him see that brief conversations can be as satisfying as long ones and that issues don't need to be dealt with across hours and hours of 'meaningful' chat.

7   Don't apply pressure to talk. If your child doesn't feel like it, the conversation is bound to be less than satisfactory anyhow. He'll feel cornered and annoyed, none of which is conducive to good communication.

If you try too hard, he'll back off, or he'll wind you up by continuing this behaviour.

What Children Learn

That communication doesn't need to be threatening, and that you can converse on a level that has nothing to do with expectations or behaviour. They will learn to develop a healthy relationship with you, based on fun as well as parenting. If you are never judgmental, and listen without criticism, they will trust you and feel confident about confiding in you. They'll also learn that it is acceptable to go into their shells from time to time, and that you are always there when they need you.

Maintenance

Allow your children times when they simply don't want to talk. If there is a sudden breakdown in communication, you might want to gently persuade your child to open up about problems he might feel he needs to hide. Show that you will love and accept him, no matter what has gone wrong, and that you have faith in his ability to get through things. Back off and leave it to him to open up when he's ready.

Organization (and a lack of it)

Many adults get through life being totally disorganized, and you can bet that many children will manage just fine without great organizational skills. Everyone's different – some people thrive on and exist in chaos; others need an ordered life in order to get through their days. The bottom line is that you may just have a naturally disorganized child, and you may simply have to put up with it. That doesn't mean, however, that you shouldn't take the opportunity to teach her some skills that will help her keep things up and running.

What to Do

1　Model the behaviour yourself. If you live in a haphazard household where everything is done spontaneously, you are unlikely to show your children that being organized is something beneficial.

2　Being disorganized is not a crime, so don't be tempted to make your child feel guilty or wrong for being the way she is. Focus on ways that could make things easier for her, but let her know you value and respect her for the way she is.

3　Teach basic time management – get her to break her day or week into manageable chunks and to plan when things are going to be done. This helps her see that a little pre-planning not only frees up time for the things she wants to do, but ensures that everything gets done – and on time.

4　Teach her how to make lists – of things to do, of articles required for various activities or classes and of things she wants to achieve. Put a pinboard in her bedroom so that she can keep her lists in full view. Even highly organized people need their memories jogged from time to time.

5　Don't be tempted to organize your child. She'll simply feel overpowered, under-respected and hen-pecked. What's worse, she'll never learn to do things for herself.

6　Let her make some mistakes and learn the hard way. If she has to miss a games session because she forgot her trainers, or if she gets a detention for failing to meet a deadline, then let her work out for herself that she needs to become more organized.

7　Show faith in her ability to organize things herself, and don't comment or make her feel stupid when she slips up. If asked, gently make some suggestions and let her know you are there to help if she needs you. In the end, however, this is one lesson she is going to have to learn herself.

What Children Learn

That they are responsible for their time, their belongings and the day-to-day organization of the parts of their lives you don't take care of. With a little guidance, they will eventually develop skills that will set them in good stead for life. They also learn, however, that it's OK not to be perfect all the time and that a haphazard approach to life is as valid as being a perfectionist.

Maintenance

Offer advice when required, continue to model and teach skills that might help them, and show faith in their ability to do things themselves. If your child suddenly becomes disorganized or scatty, it may be that she has too much on her mind for her to focus on little things (a normal reaction, even for adults). See if you can get to the root of the problem and work out some solutions together.

Playground Problems

There are dozens of scenarios for this type of problem. Your child may be experiencing some bullying (*see page 116*), being a bit of a bully himself, falling out with friends (*see page 152*), asserting his authority by being bossy, or even being left out of games and fun. Whatever the cause, and this needs to be worked out, this is something that needs to be dealt with by your child. You can offer support, love, faith and ideas, but ultimately your child will need to learn to fight his battles for himself.

What to Do

1   First of all, you may be witness to problems, which
    will give you the ideal starter conversation: 'I noticed
    that you were sitting alone a lot. Is there something
    worrying you?', or 'I saw you fighting with some
    bigger boys. Was there a problem?' Let your child
    express his concerns without judging or blaming him,
    whether or not you think the problem was caused by
    his behaviour.

2   Ask your child what he thinks he could do about it.
    Listen to his suggestions and show approval and faith.
    If they seem unrealistic, don't comment negatively.
    Just suggest a few of your own and ask his opinion.

3   Remember that playground battles, tiffs and trouble
    are all part of growing up. Throw any bunch of
    different children together and you are bound to see
    some sparks fly. What your child learns is that he
    needs to negotiate, compromise, understand, forgive
    and exercise some patience in relationships with his
    friends and peers.

4   If your child feels under pressure or has negative self-
    beliefs or low self-respect, he may feel inadequate and
    that he doesn't fit in. This can cause all sorts of
    behaviours, from being bossy (to exert a little power
    over his life and surroundings), sulking, falling out
    with friends and even aggression. Make sure your
    child feels good about himself (*see page 69*) and that
    he is able to express his emotions. If he can get them
    out, analyse them and see that all emotions are
    normal, he'll feel a lot more in control and able to
    cope with daily setbacks and set-tos.

5   Don't try to sort out your child's problems for him by
    intervening. If there is serious bullying, you may need
    to speak to a teacher or another person in authority.

For the most part, however, it's important for your child to see not only that problems can be solved, but that he can do it himself.

6 Try to remember that spats between children usually blow over quickly. Things that upset you may actually be trivial events in your child's life and he will be able to cope with them easily. If you show undue concern, you may well build it up into something it isn't.

What Children Learn

That they have the power to negotiate their own relationships, and that they can work through their problems and feelings in order to do this. They will know they have your full support, love and respect; it will teach them to respect others and, more importantly, to respect themselves. They will also see that there are ups and downs in life and in relationships, and that it is possible to overcome the bad times and take things back to an even footing.

Maintenance

If your child is suddenly experiencing problems in the playground, you may need to look at whether there are factors in his life making him stressed or unhappy. Encourage him to express his feelings and validate them. He may just need to feel that he is being heard, and that he still and always will at least have your love and attention. Remember that children often magnify small problems and some of these may be down to perception rather than reality. He may claim that he has 'no friends', for example, when you know this simply isn't the case. Just reinforce your faith in him and he'll get through it eventually.

Pouting and Whining

Children who pout and whine are likely to have had some success using this method to get what they want in the past. All children have to face disappointment and times when things do not go the way they planned. What they need to learn, however, is to experience their feelings and find ways to move on. Some children whine and pout because it is the only thing that works – they feel overpowered and perhaps that they have no choice in their lives, so they whine and complain until they get what they want. Very few parents can tolerate pouting and whining for long periods so an awful lot give in.

What to Do

1　Very simply, don't give in. Ignore the behaviour and focus instead on the emotion or problem causing it: 'I can see you're upset. What's the problem?' and then 'Now we've worked out what it is, what do you want to do about solving it?' Offer assistance so she can work out a solution, but do not give in.

2　Make sure your child has a healthy self-respect. Whining and pouting children are not behaving in a way that shows this. Avoid losing your temper, name-calling or punishing her for pouting. This will only exacerbate problems with self-esteem and self-respect. Instead, show some faith: 'You're a clever girl. There are lots of ways to get what you want and this isn't one of them. What else can you do?'

3　Help your child to verbalize her feelings. Say things like: 'I know you're disappointed', 'You must be very upset', 'You seem sad'. Then show understanding: 'It's often difficult to accept that we can't always get our own way and I would be sad, too.' But then move on.

4   Offer choices to snap your child out of the behaviour: 'Do you want to come with me now and go the supermarket or do you want to stay behind with a baby-sitter?' Chances are she'll welcome the opportunity to move forward without losing face, and to show some power herself by making a choice.
5   Watch the way you behave when you are let down. Do you sulk or pout or complain? Children do mirror what they see, and it helps to be a good role model.

What Children Learn

Children learn that things don't always go their way and that they need to learn to cope with feelings of disappointment. They will also see that experiencing feelings is fine, but expressing them with negative behaviour isn't going to change the outcome, no matter what. They will realize that you love and respect them, and will always support them, but that you will not be blackmailed into changing your mind.

Practising (instruments, etc.)

In a heavily scheduled lifestyle, instrument, sport, dance or any other practice can seem like one more pressure for children. It's not surprising that they resist the things they don't absolutely love. And that is the crux of this problem. If your child doesn't want to practise, is he actually getting any satisfaction or enjoyment from undertaking this activity? Many children are enrolled in activities because their parents feel they will enhance their lives, their prospects of success and their kiddie portfolio in some way. There's also the issue of keeping up with the Joneses. If every other kid is doing it, you don't want yours to miss out. Some parents also want their children to take part in things they wish they had had the opportunity to do when they were young. Children often change their minds. They try something, decide they don't like it and want to give up.

What to Do

1   First of all, respect your child's likes and dislikes. Piano lessons might have seemed like a great idea, but your child may find he simply doesn't enjoy it, that he has no natural ability or talent or that it is taking up too much time. Don't encourage your child to give up immediately. Agree (and it's best to do this at the outset of any new activity) to try something for a given period of time (a term, for example, or in the case of an instrument, until they reach the first grade). Often things are difficult in the beginning because there is a lot to take on board and results are not always instantly forthcoming. Give your child some time to settle in and find his feet before allowing a change.

2   Try to encourage your children to choose their own activities or musical instruments. Your ideas might not match theirs. If they choose it, they are much more likely to stick it out.

3   Try to ensure your expectations are realistic. Activities should be fun and rewarding. If they become yet another pressure, it's not surprising that kids don't want to continue. It may be that you have a talented child who could do with some pushing, but do it in a positive way, and ensure he feels rewarded for his effort and is aware of his gift.

4   Don't let practising overwhelm your child's schedule. If it's taking too much time, consider cutting back or dropping the activity.

5   Make practising a regular part of your routine. It's not only easier to fit in when you have a good schedule, but children end up doing it out of habit, which means less fuss.

6 Give your child some choices wherever possible: 'Do you want to practise now or after homework?' You are making it clear that it has to be done, but they have some say in the proceedings.

7 Admit to your child that practising can be boring, but focus on the positive outcome and take pride in every little achievement on the way – a new dance step, a back flip, a song mastered. If he thinks he is getting somewhere, and that his efforts are being recognized, he is more likely to continue.

8 Show an interest in what he is doing. If he feels isolated from the rest of the family while practising, perhaps you can become more involved. Sit near him, or organize a family concert or show. Let him know that you all take pride in his achievements.

What Children Learn

If your child is given choices about how he fills his time, he will know that you respect him and will take pride in his decisions. He will also learn that practising can be boring, but that it is the only way to improve. It's a tough lesson, but one that everyone has to learn. We only get better when we work on things. Children also learn that they have the right to change their minds, but only after they have given things a try. This teaches them to motivate themselves, to give things a proper chance before giving up, and it also helps them to develop a little staying power. If it still doesn't work out, they have choices. Most children also learn that it is great to have hobbies and outside interests. Practising may be the thin edge of the fun wedge, but getting better at something can be enormously rewarding and gain them lots of attention and pride.

Maintenance

If things slip, re-evaluate what your child is doing and make sure he's not overloaded. Help him with some scheduling to make it easier to fit in what he wants to do. Consider that it might be the wrong activity for your child. Not every child will make a pianist, a dancer or an athlete, no matter how hard he works. Give your child the space to change his mind.

Pre-schoolers and Primary School Children

It's normal for children in this age group to exhibit a wide range of behaviours. These include:

- tantrums when things don't go their own way
- aggression when they are angry and do not have the maturity to cope with conflicting emotions
- persistent questioning
- whining
- a fear of new experiences
- loss of concentration
- nightmares
- normal complaints about friends, siblings, discipline and, of course, school

Pre-school children are constantly trying new activities and becoming more independent. This can be stimulating, exhausting, frightening and exhilarating. These confused feelings are often reflected in their behaviour, which can swing between the various emotions. They are also learning to understand the world around them and their role within it. As babies and toddlers, they tend to believe they are the centre of their world. It can be a rude shock to find that they aren't as important as they thought they were. Of course, they will always be as important to you, but their view of life inevitably changes as they mature. There might be a new baby on the scene; they are learning that they have to share their toys; nappies, cots and dummies disappear. They are also beginning to see that they are responsible for their own actions, and that there are rules that need to be learned and adhered to. These responses are all normal, and part of development.

School-age children come into contact with a much wider and more frightening world, so they are bound to have worries and fears. They are also leaving behind the comfort of having a parent or carer by their side almost constantly, and probably a favourite blanket or stuffed animal as well. At school, they begin to master simple and then more complex tasks, which involve reasoning and logical thinking. A huge range of skills are developed, and for the first time they may experience peer competition and a need for intense concentration, while becoming more self-aware and conscious of differences, performance and achievement.

In both cases, be aware of the changes your child is facing, and be understanding. Help her find words to express the various emotions she is feeling; she will feel more secure if she knows that not only is it acceptable to feel that way, but that there are actually words to describe it. Children in this age group will probably need a lot of affection and comfort to reassure them that, despite the vast changes taking place in their world, you still love them, value them and respect them, and that home remains the sanctuary it always was. Show tolerance when your child exhibits unacceptable behaviour, but don't hesitate to teach something more appropriate. These are formative years and your child will be a sponge for information and learning. Habits are often set at these very early ages. You will do yourself and your child a great favour if you spend time explaining:

- the reasons why there are rules and codes of behaviour
- why there is a need to conform some of the time
- why some behaviour is unacceptable and how it affects others
- how they will feel a lot happier and more secure if they fall in line with what is expected of them

Don't hesitate to put forward your expectations and justify them, and help her learn respect for herself and others. Spend time with your child. While she is absorbing so much of the world around her and learning crucial lessons, it is important that you are able to convey your own philosophies to help her make sense of it all and put it into context.

Take pleasure in the steps your child is taking towards adolescence and, ultimately, independence. Every achievement, effort and milestone represents a lesson or an experience that your child has learned. It all comes together to provide her with a foundation for emotional growth and development, and a framework upon which she will rely to make decisions, choose paths, find self-respect and grow up to be happy and healthy.

Procrastinating

Let's face it – we all procrastinate. How many of us have drawers that need emptying, cupboards that need tidying, bills to be paid, post to deal with ...? In an ideal world, we'd all get on with things and get them done instantly, for there is no better satisfaction than completing a task that has been niggling at the back of our minds. But the reality? In many cases it doesn't happen because we procrastinate. We choose different activities to fill our time and put it on the backburner for later ... and later.

So try to show a little understanding if you have a procrastinator on your hands. Obviously, we all want to get across the message that it's better to do things today than put them off till tomorrow, but if it's not fun, there's little in it for them.

What to Do

1   Make the activity rewarding for them. They'll have little sense of the relief they will feel when it's done, so don't bother going down that route. Instead, offer tangible rewards – a little time off to do whatever

they please when their homework is done, or the right to dictate their own evening if they can get it done before dinner. A great big star on a chart for cleaning a room, dealing with that pile of toys or making a phone call. Show them that you recognize their effort and don't hesitate to reward them. There are arguments against this philosophy, but I call it positive reinforcement (*see page 58*). You are rewarding the effort you want to see.

2   Some children procrastinate in an attempt to get their parents' notice. They know it's bound to lead to cajoling, nagging, bribing, encouraging – all of which represents a little attention in their eyes. If your child fails to do something, don't hound him. Let him pay the consequences of his actions. If he doesn't get the homework done, then he can pay the price at school the next day.

3   Many of us resist tasks because they seem too daunting, and that goes for children too. Teach them how to break things into manageable chunks: studying, cleaning, practising, etc., so that it appears more achievable. Have rewarding breaks in between.

4   Sometimes children procrastinate because they are afraid of failing, not living up to your expectations or messing things up. Show faith in their ability to get things right, and commiserate if they don't. Let them see you are proud of every attempt to get things done.

5   Give choices about when things will be done. Make it clear that it *will* be done but that you will respect their right to choose when: 'Do you want to do it before tea when I can help you out, or do you want to do it after tea when your mum will be home?'

6   Point out the consequences of procrastination. Children will never have the luxury of a free weekend if they don't clear the decks. No one likes the feeling

of something hanging over them. Point it out to them, and show that it's much easier to relax and enjoy life without unmet obligations.

7   Teach some basic time management (*see page 203*), to help your child organize his time better.

What Children Learn

Children learn that leaving something to the last minute or letting it lurk in the background of their lives can be an uncomfortable feeling. It's much more satisfying to get things done. The fact is that some things in life *need* to be done regularly and they will see that it's better to face them and work through them. They will develop planning and organization skills and learn to balance their time so they can fit everything in. They will also learn what happens when they do procrastinate!

Maintenance

Chronic procrastination can mean that your child is over-scheduled and simply does not have the resources to deal with everything he needs to get done. In this situation, it's much easier for him to put it off. Help him plan his time and drop some activities if it's all too much. Remember that some people work better under pressure and produce their best results when up against a deadline. It may be that your child is one of these people. Respect that. Make sure, however, that procrastination isn't being used as an attempt to wind you up. Let him see that you will support him, but you aren't there to rescue him.

Rebellion

Children rebel when they feel cornered, pressurized and powerless. They do so to strike out and define their own identities and purpose, to exert some power over their environment and their lives, to show independence and to resist attempts by others to mould them into something they do not believe they are. First of all, remember that a rebellious child is showing spirit and this is something to be applauded. You'd much rather have the occasional rebel than a child who is meekly obedient and allows anyone to walk over her. Mild rebellion is an acceptable way of showing unique characteristics – your child may decide to dress differently, dye her hair, play wacky music, for example. It often shows great strength of character and self-belief to live their lives outside the norm and this type of creative approach to life may well get them far. Remember that different doesn't necessarily mean rebellious. It's important to respect the fine line between healthy rebellion of the accepted norm and rebellion against you and/or other figures of authority.

What to Do

1   If you have genuine rebellion problems, look at your own parenting. Are your expectations too high? Are you trying to force your child to be someone she is not? Are you showing respect for her views and her way of doing things? Do you overpower and offer few choices? If children feel pressured or powerless, they will undoubtedly rebel. Interestingly, some of the most over-disciplined children behave beautifully while under the eyes of their parents but go completely off the rails once they are on their own. Why? Because they have never learned to make their own decisions and never had any respect for their ability to do so. When they are finally given the opportunity to be themselves, the freedom can be terrifying.

2   Teach your children to respect important rules and to realize that some of them might be arbitrary, but that they are there for a reason. There's nothing wrong

with pointing out what's wrong with regulations from time to time, but the bottom line is that they are going to need to learn to respect them.

3   Make sure your child feels accepted for who she is, and feels confident expressing herself in whatever ways she finds appropriate. If she thinks there is something wrong with her ideas, dress code or whatever, she might as well give up trying to please you and go the whole hog with the rebellious approach to everything.

4   Consider the fact that your child might want to shock you. She might think you are so intransigent in your views that you need a little shaking up. She may feel she cannot get her message across any other way. Show her you are willing to listen, adapt, understand, respect and compromise.

5   Watch out for over-control. If you try to control every aspect of her life, she is bound to rebel on at least one front. All children need to be in control of their own lives to some extent. Give her some choices and some freedom. If you show faith in her ability to make the right decisions (not the decisions you think she should make but the decisions that are right for her), she's more likely to rise to the challenge.

6   Don't punish rebellion or you'll only lock horns. Get to the root of the motivation that caused the behaviour and be prepared to listen and compromise. If your child perceives things to be unfair, too tightly controlled, overwhelming or whatever, then for her they are and that's all that matters. Try to find a way to reach a medium ground that keeps you all happy.

What Children Learn

That being outside the norm is acceptable. That you respect her differences, and even love her for it. Children do need to see, however, that putting up a wall and doing their own thing only alienates them. They will learn that communication, making their views and opinions heard, is the only way to make changes that will make their lives easier and happier.

Maintenance

Rebellion is often a last-ditch attempt to get much-needed attention and power. Don't ignore it. If your child suddenly becomes rebellious, take the time to analyse what she is resisting and work with her to compromise and make changes where necessary. Like all behaviour, rebellion is your child's way of sending you a message that all is not well. Ensure you respect her and show faith in her ability to exert some power over her life and make choices that will make her happy.

Respect, Lack of

Lack of respect usually comes from only one thing – the fact that children are not respected themselves. So, if you show little respect for your child, his ideas, who he is, his viewpoint, his interests and enthusiasms, his friends, his unique personality, and everything else about him, he's not likely to return the favour. Respect shows understanding and appreciation. It isn't enough just to love your child. If you don't respect who they are, they will never have the self-respect necessary to find the best course in life.

What to Do

1 Take steps to earn your child's respect by respecting him. Show delight, approval and interest in the things he does. That doesn't mean rewarding 'bad' behaviour; it simply means focusing on your child's

strengths and unique characteristics and letting him
know that you value them and him. Listen to your
child. Give him time and concentrate on what he is
saying. Take the opportunity to discuss what he has
to say and give him credit.

2 Be consistent. Nothing undermines respect more than
being flaky. If you give in, change your mind, break
promises, change the rules and lash out with unfair
punishments, he is not going to develop respect.

3 Show respect for other people. Mutual respect is a
great foundation for friendships, working
relationships and loving relationships. If he sees it in
action, he is more likely to mimic it.

4 Remember that respect is earned. Your child is under
no obligation to respect you. You have to give him
reasons to do so and that comes down to:

- consistent parenting
- realistic expectations
- active listening
- fairness
- respect for him
- respect for yourself and others
- a sound discipline policy based on fair principles
- an ability to accept and own up to your own
  mistakes, and to accept theirs.

5 Treat your children as you would like to be treated
yourself. This fosters mutual respect and
communication, which is crucial.

6 Take the time to explain why you are doing things
and why you believe things should be a certain way.
Don't use the old excuse that 'it's the way things are
done'. If you can show a reason why you are
determined for certain things to happen, your child

will respect your stand. Adopting a sheep-like
mentality will do nothing to gain your child's respect.

7   Make honesty not only your policy, but a family
    policy.

What Children Learn

Respect is the foundation of discipline in all walks of life.
If your child learns it early on, he will apply it, where
appropriate, for the rest of his life. He will learn self-respect,
and see the importance of respect in any relationship.

Maintenance

Once gained, it's difficult to lose respect, unless you do
something out of character and unacceptable. If you make
a mistake, admit it and apologize. Be humble when
necessary and never let your pride stand in the way of a
good relationship. If you show injustice or act unfairly,
again, admit it and move on. You can maintain respect as
long as you are consistent, honest and sincere.

Rude Behaviour

Some rudeness in children is undoubtedly unconscious –
a throwaway comment, a quick retort, a nasty comment
may be nothing more than an unintended, uncontrolled
instant reaction. Other times, rudeness is designed to hurt
you or others, or to show that they will not be controlled.

What to Do

1   First of all, make sure you are not rude to them. It's
    easy to say things in the heat of the moment, and to
    show disrespect. Once again, if you model the
    behaviour, they are likely to follow suit. Double
    standards will never work in any healthy
    relationship. Similarly, look at how you treat other

people. If you are rude to the cleaner, the bank clerk, the frustrating call centre employee at the other end of the line, or even your partner, your child will think it is acceptable behaviour, particularly when one is frustrated or angry.

2   Overlook or ignore rudeness if it appears to be designed to get a response. Pay attention to positive behaviour instead.

3   If the rudeness is consistent, ask some questions: 'I can see you are feeling very angry because you aren't normally rude to me. Is there something bothering you?' Let them know you have taken note of the behaviour and that you don't find it acceptable, but put the ball back in their court so that they can examine their own motivation.

4   Young children may genuinely not realize they are being rude. Gently explain that it is not polite to speak or behave that way. If you don't explain, they'll never know.

5   Put rudeness on the family meeting agenda, and ask your children for reasons why people might be rude. Ask them how they feel when someone is rude to them. Then agree an anti-rudeness policy. You haven't put them on the spot by saying that you have noticed their behaviour in particular, but they'll get the message and be forced to look at their motivation and its consequences.

What Children Learn

That rudeness is not acceptable and that nothing is ever gained by being rude. They'll also learn that being kind and loving is a much better way to attract friends and maintain good relationships.

Maintenance

If your child continues with rude, belligerent behaviour, give her a warning and set a pre-arranged penalty. Make it clear that it is unacceptable. You aren't going to be drawn into an argument, or lock horns, or give attention to this type of behaviour. Don't say a word. Hold up that yellow card and make your feelings known. She then has a choice about how to behave, and she'll pay the consequences if she continues to show disrespect (*see also 'Respect, lack of', page 219*).

Shopping

Shopping with children is designed to try the patience of a saint. Some children love it and have huge expectations about what a shopping trip might entail, usually treats. Others despise it and moan and complain the entire time, robbing the experience of every ounce of potential pleasure. The problem is that shopping trips do need to take place and your children are going to have to learn to put up with it.

What to Do

1   Make your expectations very clear at the outset. You plan to go to X number of shops, some of which will be boring for them. You plan to be gone X number of hours. You will, however, take time to visit X number of their favourite shops, and you are prepared to turn 20 minutes over to each one of them (buy yourself a cup of coffee and lean against the wall). Make clear how much money they will have to spend, if any, or if you have any intention of purchasing something for them other than vests and knickers. If you plan to buy them a treat, make it clear at the outset that you have

a budget and that a choice needs to be made within that bracket.

2   For younger children, break up the experience with lots of stops at fun shops. Bring along a bag of toys and snacks to occupy him, and arrange a few treats along the way – lunch at McDonalds, for example, a trip to the play park or an ice-cream cone. Talk to your child as you travel, telling him what you are doing next and what is in it for him. Reward a successful shopping trip with a pre-arranged treat.

3   Let older children have a little freedom. Agree to meet them at a certain point and time and be sure they have a watch. Even if they don't have money to spend, most children will relish this little bit of freedom.

4   Try to make it fun. Chat, laugh, point things out, and get your children involved in choosing things and paying at the till. If you go through the shops with grim determination, no one is likely to gain any pleasure from the experience.

What Children Learn

That not everything in life is necessarily fun, or will live up to their expectations. They will learn patience and see that it is always rewarded. They also learn that even the most laborious of experiences can be fun if you approach it with the right attitude.

Maintenance

If your child resists shopping and will not be convinced otherwise, leave him with a friend or at the baby-sitting centre. He may well decide that he'd rather be with you than farmed out. Remember to offer rewards for effort; if he feels something is worth his while, he will undoubtedly join in.

Shyness

Shyness is often more an issue for parents than it is for children. Many parents feel they have somehow failed because their children aren't sparkling little balls of entertainment and overt intelligence. Some children simply are shy. They are quieter, feel less need for interaction and are daunted by new people and situations. And there is nothing wrong with that. What you do need to get across is the issue of being polite – answering questions, looking people in the eye when they speak, and responding in the appropriate manner to new people. But don't expect anything more than that. If your child suddenly becomes shy or has a fear of new situations and people, it may be that she lacks confidence or self-belief.

What to Do

1 Whatever you do, don't be tempted to label your child as 'shy'. Although there is nothing wrong with *being* shy, it can be something that sticks with her for life and becomes a self-fulfilling prophecy.

2 Don't be tempted to speak for your children or cajole them into interacting when they don't want to. Give them a respectful silence in which to answer questions or speak for themselves; if they fail to do so, carry on, so that they don't feel embarrassed.

3 Make sure your child feels comfortable and accepted for being the way she is. Show her that it is equally valid to be introverted and quiet as it is to be a noisy extrovert!

4 Don't try to force your children into situations that are daunting for them. Take things slowly and applaud every step along the way. Some children simply develop at different stages to others, and you may need to exercise some patience.

5   Make sure your child feels confident enough to express herself, and that her views, opinions and ideas are always taken seriously. Many shy children are younger siblings who are used to having the air bashed out of them every time they open their mouths. Pay equal attention to shy members of the family and give them an equal voice, even if it means forbidding interruptions from other siblings until she has finished!

6   Is your child being quiet or shy to wind you up? Is there a power struggle in which she is gaining some ground by doing something she knows will get a reaction? Lay off entirely and let her be herself. If she comes out of her 'shell', so be it. If she doesn't, maybe she's happy there.

What Children Learn

That it is acceptable to be themselves, no matter how different that might be to the rest of the family. They also see that they are loved for who they are, rather than what their parents think they should be. Finally, they will see that they don't need to be pushed into situations they find uncomfortable. They can do things at the right time for them and that's OK.

Sibling Rivalry

Unlike the ties between parents and children, the connection between siblings is a horizontal one. That is, siblings exist on the same plane – as peers, more or less equals. Although one may be stronger or more dominant than the others, brothers and sisters rarely exert the kind of power and authority over one another that parents hold over their children. Nor are there rules, codes of behaviour for different stages of life or biblical commandments mandating siblings to respect and honour one another as they must respect and honour parents. As a result, they are freer, more open and generally more honest with one another than they are with parents, and less fearful of punishment or rejection. As children, they say what is on their minds without censoring their words or concerning themselves about the long-term effects of their emotions on one another. Even as adults, many siblings speak more bluntly to each other than they dare to friends or colleagues.

It is perfectly normal, natural and appropriate for parents to have different feelings towards each of their children, and to treat those children differently. The challenge they always face is to appreciate what is unique about each child and to show that appreciation in a balanced way so that, over the course of years, all children feel equally loved and valued. Parents fail in that challenge when the line between different treatment and preferential treatment becomes muddied and, without ever realizing it, they begin to slip from one to the other.

Unintentionally, the most achieving child, the most affectionate one, the first born or the last, the one most like or unlike a parent or relative can move from a position of equality with other children to one of receiving or seeming to receive special attention. Parents may not be aware of slipping from a normal course of treating children differently to giving one preferential treatment. Siblings, however, whether children, adolescents or adults, are highly sensitive to such slips. They pick up signals of favouritism not only from the way parents behave towards them but also from parental behaviour towards their brothers and sisters. Young children monitor their parents' treatment of their siblings, just as they monitor their own treatment, and that relationship of parent to siblings becomes as important as the relationship of parent to self.

It is certainly true that what young children label favouritism may be far from the real thing.

But herein lies the crux of the problem. It's perception rather than reality that colours a sibling relationship. If a child perceives that he is being treated less fairly or not getting enough, even if parents are scrupulously fair, he will feel disempowered and more likely to initiate rivalry.

Sibling rivalry is exhausting for everyone involved. Often, siblings are the only outlet stressed children have to exert control, lash out, scrap, fight, bicker, taunt, tease and harass. You will often see your child exhibiting horrendous behaviour with his siblings and it can be a sign that things are just too much.

Although books advise parents not to compare their children, but to view each only as an individual, most parents find it almost impossible not to make some comparisons. It is when the comparisons turn into labels used to define and pigeonhole children that they may become problematic. Labels, stuck on in early childhood, become part of the internal image children have of themselves, later to be incorporated into the roles they assume with each other and in the world outside the family.

What to Do

1 Sensitive parenting can restore the balance and, in many cases, prevent serious rivalry from taking hold.

2 Make each of your children feel special. Older or younger, every child needs to feel that he is as important as anyone else in the family. If one child thinks his sibling is held in higher esteem by his parents, jealousy will arise. Do your best to listen to each of your children and respond to them positively.

3 Show enthusiasm for all your children's achievements. You may find that you are less excited about your younger child's milestones (such as his first step, his first word) than you were with your older child. It is not that you love him less, but that there is not the same novelty. If you do feel this way, try not to let it show. Your youngest children need you to be interested.

4 Give each of your children responsibility. Resist the trap of giving your oldest child all the household chores. There is no reason why he has to do everything, just because of his age. His younger siblings can also help – by tidying toys, for example. And the oldest child does not need to take his younger siblings with him whenever he goes out to play.

5 Respect all your children. Every child has the same psychological need to be loved and accepted by his parents, no matter what his position in the family.

He has feelings and ideas that he wants to express. He has a right to receive respect and to be taken seriously, whether he is the youngest, middle or oldest child.

6   When rivalry declines into violence or regular bickering, it's usually best to ignore it. Children need to learn to sort out their problems, negotiate and find a happy middle ground. If you constantly intervene, they will always expect you to.

7   Make kindness to siblings a family policy and reward all efforts towards this goal. Children will soon see that it's easier to get along than it is to waste energy fighting a useless cause.

8   Remember that children will lash out at each other from time to time, and it's completely normal. Try to teach them other ways of relieving frustration and anger (*see page 92*), and make it clear that it is not acceptable to treat others in ways that they would not like to be treated themselves. Above all, show some understanding and patience. Sibling rivalry occurs in almost every family at some point or another. You need to look at places where the balance of power or attention may have shifted, or when one or more of your children needs some extra love and time.

What Children Learn

Children will learn that it is acceptable to be different, and that the differences between them and their siblings don't need to be a point of conflict. Through this, they learn tolerance of other people and their behaviour. They also learn how to be resourceful and sort out problems for themselves, through negotiation or other means. Most importantly, however, they learn that you love all of them unconditionally and that there is no favouritism. One child may be more needy than another at certain times, but in the end, everyone gets their fair share of the attention, and there is plenty of love to go around.

Maintenance

Watch out for times when you may be exacerbating the problem by unwittingly favouring another child or showing him more attention. Ensure, too, that your relations with your partner are healthy, uncompetitive and respectful. Children tend to mirror behaviour they see around them. Stress cooperation, which focuses on the uniqueness and differences of every child, rather than competition or comparing. If you consistently reiterate that every child is loved for being himself, the problem should ease.

Sports and Competition

Competition is part of life. Every child needs to know how to deal with competitive colleagues and friends. In fact, competition can be healthy, providing the drive and stimulation to finish a task and to do one's best. It's an aspect of your child's life that can be healthy in the short term, raising energy levels and stimulating the senses. But, like everything else, constant competition is stressful and exhausting. If your child is highly competitive, she may be trying to live up to your expectations, or demanding too much of herself in order to prove her self-worth.

What to Do

1 Children need to make choices in order to have some control over their environment. If they feel stressed by competition, they should have the choice not to take part in recreational activities they don't find rewarding.

2 Look at your own expectations. Are you putting pressure on your child to succeed? Examine the

reasons why. Ensure that you aren't living through your children and claiming their successes as your own. So what if your child comes last in the swimming gala? It's no reflection of your parenting and at least she had the courage to try. Make her proud of that.

3   Parents who push their children to excel cause them to doubt their own worth. If children feel they haven't 'achieved' their parents expectations at home, they are driven to do so in another environment, namely school or sports. Similarly, later in life, children who face intense competition can experience debilitating stress, disillusionment and burnout. They often realize that they have been pushed and been pushing for something that simply doesn't exist – perfection.

4   Children often feel overwhelmed by competition, which is why it is extremely important to ensure that your child takes part in plenty of non-demanding activities, which act as an outlet rather than a source of stress. Being alone is one thing that can help, for children cannot be pressured when they are in their own space.

5   Remember that activities should be fun. If your son spends his weekends on the football pitch and your daughter in the gym, they'll need to use this all-important leisure time to relax, enjoy and let off steam. If you place too much pressure on their fun time, you'll increase the competitive element and, through that, the stress load.

6   Encourage a healthy level of competition, but praise effort and individual progress rather than winning or being the best. If a child feels unthreatened by competition at home, and feels that her efforts are being recognized, she won't feel the need to overachieve in other areas of her life.

7   Ensure your children don't feel they have to compete for your love or attention. If they learn this lesson early on, they'll be more likely to believe that they have to compete for everything in life. Their home environment should always be non-threatening, uncompetitive, safe and loving.

8   By all means share your expectations, but make them relevant and realistic, and don't apply pressure to see that they are realized. All children benefit from having goals, targets and an understanding of why it is important to be the best they can be. That doesn't mean being the best of all, however; it simply means making the most of individual talents to carve a niche for themselves in life.

9   Try to take the competition out of the family dynamic. Reward and celebrate effort and achievement in all walks of life, ensuring that your child sees her individuality – and her individual strengths and weaknesses – as something positive. If your children all feel they are treated as individuals, and respected for their differences, they will feel less need to compete with one another or, indeed, with others.

What Children Learn

Competition is healthy to some degree and children learn to push themselves to be the best they can be. They also learn to accept defeat and disappointment as part of life, rather than personal slights. This is a crucial lesson. Only one person can ever be the best. Children also learn that the home is a competition-free zone and that they are loved, valued and respected for who they are, never what they need to achieve.

Maintenance

At family meetings, discuss areas of your children's lives that have become overcompetitive and try to work out solutions. Try to make sure that each of your children feels valued and respected for who she is. Never compare your children, even in a positive light, as comparison almost always leads to a sense of competition (*see also 'Sibling Rivalry', page 226*).

Stealing

It's normal for all children to steal something once or twice in their lives. It is important that you don't overreact and label your child a thief, something that could stay with him for a very long time. If stealing becomes a problem, it's important that you look at what might be happening in your child's life to prompt such action. If he is taking things because it is the only way he'll ever get them (money, CDs, toys, etc.), then you may need to work out if his basic needs are being covered by pocket money or other sources. Ensure that your analysis of his needs is realistic.

Stealing also takes place in order to punish someone, by taking something they love or value in order to hurt them. In a way, it's a bit of a revenge attack. Older children and teenagers may steal in order to gain the approval of their peers, or for the thrill factor. In any of these cases, it's important to separate the crime from the child, and work out what is driving this behaviour.

What to Do

1   First of all, have a good policy in place in your home, where children are brought up to respect one another's property and to value their own.

2   Find ways to ensure that your children feel loved and included. If they have problems or are angry (*see page 92*), they need to be able to express that and work on solutions with a caring parent. Revenge attacks suggest feelings of isolation, a child acting spitefully because he feels he has no other choice.

3   Ensure your children have the basic level of accessories and gear that their friends have. If they constantly feel left out or different, and you don't seem to understand or appreciate their position, they may steal out of desperation. That does mean giving in to consumerism (*see page 187*), but ensuring your child is not put in the position of feeling unable to join in with his friends.

4   If your child does steal, don't be too harsh. Don't corner him by saying things like: 'Did you steal XXXX?' You'll only end up causing panic and encouraging a lie. Admit that you know he took something and that you would like it returned, replaced or paid for. Then ask how he would like to do this. Encourage him to tell the truth. If you respond negatively, you can count on the fact that he won't be truthful again.

5   Make it clear that you will always love your child, no matter what he does, but that you will never be put in the position of rescuing him or covering for him. He is, ultimately, accountable for his own actions and he will have to take responsibility when he makes mistakes.

6   Younger children who take things should be put in the position of the victim: 'I can see you have taken Luke's toy. We'd better return it. He's probably very sad without it and worried that he might have lost it.' Your child will see that it is wrong to take things that belong to other people because it causes hurtful feelings.

7   Teach your children to own up to their mistakes. The best way to do this is to show understanding for the embarrassment or distress they might feel, but be firm about the need always to rectify our own errors.

What Children Learn

They learn that mistakes can be rectified by taking personal responsibility. They will see that they won't lose your love and respect, and that they are not 'bad' people. They will learn to be honest about problems and come to you for advice and some help finding a solution, rather than relying on stealing to get what they want or need.

Maintenance

If your children continue to steal, you will need to work out what is driving their behaviour. Are they getting enough attention? Do they feel loved and valued and able to express their feelings openly? Is something draining their resources, such as a drug habit? Have they found themselves in with a crowd where stealing is part of the curriculum? Whatever the case, keep the communication open and honest. Don't blame or label your child. Show faith in his decision to do what is right, and be there to help him get through it.

Stubbornness

An admirable quality in adult negotiation, perhaps, but in children stubbornness can be downright maddening. Why are children stubborn? Probably for the same reason that adults are – they dig in their heels because they do not feel secure enough to let someone else be right. They feel they always have to be right or in control, or their glass house of confidence will be shattered. They may also know that they are wrong and, rather than admit it, they become intransigent for fear of discovery. It takes a brave person to admit they are wrong, that someone else might have a better idea or that there is a different way of doing things.

What to Do

1   If you have a stubborn child on your hands, try to give her an out clause. This is simply a way to leave the argument or situation without losing face. Parents can offer this by suggesting a change of scene or saying something like: 'I know you are annoyed and I'll definitely consider your point of view. Now, how about we go and feed the ducks in the park/have a biscuit/do some painting, etc.?' As long as the child doesn't feel she's lost a battle and that you are considering the options, perhaps, or willing to overlook the locked horns, she is much more likely to give in. Many children do not want to give in because they have effectively 'lost' a battle. It doesn't need to be perceived that way. Explain that you understand why she feels so strongly about something, and show admiration for her determination. Then change the subject, the scene, the room, anything, and suggest moving on.

2   Show respect for her position, but don't give in: 'That's a good point and I can see you are very determined for things to be this way. I'll certainly give it some thought.' In this way she hasn't lost anything in particular because you have validated her viewpoint and offered to consider her position.

3   Offer choices, so that your child feels she can make another decision without losing face. If it's her way or yours, she's definitely going to stand her ground. But if there are other alternatives on offer, she might leap at them to get out of an untenable position.

4   Make sure your child has self-respect and doesn't feel threatened by other people doing things differently. Everyone needs to learn to accept other people's points of view and they need to acquire the grace to do that. Make it easy. Show respect for her position. When she's right, when she has a better idea or way of doing things, when her point of view is probably more realistic than yours, admit it. If you are always right, she'll think she is too. And the result is a power struggle that no one can win.

5   Let things go her way when you can. She needs to feel she has some power and influence as well. She'll be much more likely to accept 'no' when it isn't the only answer on offer.

What Children Learn

That stubbornness often leads to being cornered, and that it's a lot easier to accept someone else's point of view or way of doing things from time to time. They'll learn that giving in doesn't mean losing face; it means learning the art of compromise. And they'll see that in a fair household, their opinions are as valid as anyone else's and will be taken seriously when appropriate.

Supermarket Syndrome

This differs from other types of shopping in one way – supermarkets appear designed to bring out the worst in children. Rows of tantalizing treats, all within hand's reach; trolleys that make great racing cars; long aisles surely designed for running up and down; lots of noise, artificial lighting and scope for trouble. Couple that with a stressed-out parent who is pressured enough to give in to some good old-fashioned begging and whining and it's trouble waiting to happen.

What to Do

1   Leave them at home, if at all possible. It saves everyone the stress and hassle factor.
2   If you do need to bring your children along, set out your expectations in advance. You expect them to walk beside the trolley and not catch lifts on it. You will allow them to take turns pushing the trolley, as long as it isn't pushed into siblings or other unwitting shoppers. You will allow them to make some choices about breakfast cereal, for example, or biscuits, fruit, cheese or crisps, but that you will be making the other decisions. And if they can manage to take all this on board and stick to the rules, they will have the opportunity to choose a treat at the end – a magazine, sticker packet, packet of sweets or crisps.
3   Involve your children as much as possible. If you've set limitations as to what they can choose and do, they'll undoubtedly be bored. But try to make it fun and teach them about food and nutrition while you are at it. Show them how to judge the ripeness of a fruit by its smell, and get them all to take a turn. Show them that a firm piece of fish is better than something flabby. Ask their opinions. Tell them about how different cereals give more energy than others, and ask them to see if they can find three of the most nutritious boxes on the shelves. When they do, ask them to choose one to buy. Let children take turns: you choose the cereal, everyone can choose a type of fruit, she chooses the cheese and so on.
4   For young children, take along a book or toy and get them to be the intermediary step between your hands and the trolley. If they show fury at being strapped in, distract them with little jobs, chatter, a treat and another toy.

5   Send them off on errands if they are old enough. Kids can be a great help if you've forgotten something aisles back.

6   Ask them to guess the price of things, and get older children to tot up the value of your shopping. Offer a prize for who is closest.

7   Get them to help with the loading and packing up. If they are involved, they'll feel important and valued and be less likely to cause trouble.

8   Praise them for a job well done and for getting through the experience. If they come away with good memories and proud feelings, the next time will be that much easier.

What Children Learn

They learn to be part of wider family responsibilities and will enjoy taking a role in helping out. They'll learn their way around shops, pick up whatever information you pass on, as well as finding ways to entertain themselves when your tricks run dry. They also learn delayed gratification and the meaning of rewards. They can earn something by behaving well, but they'll have to wait to the very end of the shop to get it!

Swearing

Swearing tends to happen when your child wants a shock reaction or because he wants to test out something he might have heard in the playground (heaven forbid it was in your house!). Children often do it because they feel 'cool'. Unfortunately, foul language is increasingly common in films and various media and it's used by people our children look up to as role models, such as sports stars, musicians and actors. Your child may use words he genuinely doesn't realize are wrong because *everyone* is using them.

What to Do

1 Explain early on in your child's life that swearing is offensive, rude and disrespectful. Make it clear that it will not be tolerated in your house and that if they choose to use it elsewhere, they must be aware that they are hurting and insulting people by doing it.

2 Don't show shock, dismay or anger if your child swears. Raise an eyebrow; perhaps ask him if he knows what it means (which always wrong-foots them) and then ignore it. It's likely that it will not be used again if the expected reaction is not given.

3 Try not to swear yourself. Double standards never come over well with kids.

4 For younger children who pick up the words, be firm. Explain that you are surprised to hear them using those words because they are very rude. Tell them that they are not allowed in your house, no matter what. Don't ignore the behaviour in young children; they may genuinely not know what they are saying and they will require guidance.

5 When children use swear words in anger, validate their feelings but let them know that you think they are clever enough to come up with something better to express their anger.

6 If your child is using swearing to get attention from you or from his peers, you need to work on his self-respect. He needs to feel loved, secure, confident and respected and you will go a long way towards stamping out problem behaviour if you can meet those needs.

7 Talk about the subject at family meetings. Ask children how they would feel if they were sworn at. Suggest other words that can replace those that offend and ways of expressing themselves that do not

involve using foul language. You might open a can of worms, but there is bound to be lots of discussion and ideas. And that's something they can draw upon when they need it.

8   Some families use a system of fining members who swear. Everyone is obliged to put a coin in a jar if they are caught. And with limited resources, this hits kids where it hurts most. It'll also keep older family members on the straight and narrow.

What Children Learn

That using offensive language does just that – it offends. They learn to express themselves in ways that do not hurt or upset other people, and to show respect.

Maintenance

If swearing becomes a real problem, you may need to arrange a penalty for this behaviour. Talk it through with your child. Explain why you think it is a problem and say that you now have no choice but to penalize him if it continues. Stick with it. Your child will much prefer to keep his freedom and treats, and swearing is usually an easy thing to give up. If it's a sudden interlude of swearing, ignore it as much as possible. Your child might be trying to wind you up and get a reaction. Try to separate the deed from the doer, and work out what might be driving that doer's behaviour.

Sweets and Treats

Most children don't think they have enough. Come to think of it, most adults feel the same way. Everyone loves treats. Used appropriately, they can be a great incentive for children to model positive behaviour. They can also be given randomly, to show generosity and a good sense of fun. Problems occur when children become obsessed with sweets and treats and begin to nag and whine in order to get what they want. Or when they are given as a show of affection: 'Look how much I love you.' This creates a situation where children learn to equate love with presents.

What to Do

1 Don't ban sweets altogether. You'll only create and feed an obsession. If you are genuinely worried about teeth and health, then keep sweets and treats for after meals. If they don't get them from you, you can be sure they'll get them from somewhere else, and they're likely to eat them at inappropriate times. It's much better to agree on an appropriate allowance of sweets.

2 Ensure that treats are not only given as rewards. They'll think they have to work for everything pleasurable in life and that's a pretty tough lesson for a youngster. There should always be occasions when they are pleasantly surprised by an unexpected treat.

3 Make sure that your children show appreciation. Too much of a good thing can cause them to take it for granted. Explain your motivation for giving a treat: 'I just thought you deserved it after all your hard work/good behaviour/helpfulness this morning/sweet smile/just because I love you.' They'll see the intent behind the gift and they will learn to appreciate the act of giving.

4 Don't use sweets or treats as bribery. They might *choose* them as a pre-arranged reward, but that's different. That is providing individual incentive and motivation for a child to do her best. If you bribe kids, you are showing disrespect because even the youngest child can sense when she is being manipulated.

5   Although discipline is an important part of parenting,
so too is teaching lessons that will stand them in good
stead for life. Make sure you impress upon them the
importance of good food, nutrition, healthy living and
caring for teeth. The sweet question will come up a
number of times and you can get your point across
without lecturing.

What Children Learn

They learn that some foods are healthy and others are not,
and how to make the correct choices. They see that treats
and sweets can be eaten in moderation, but that too much
of a good thing may mean a painful trip to the dentist.
Children learn to see treats as something to work towards
(a reward), but also as something that can be offered
simply to make someone's day. They learn to appreciate,
but most of all they learn generosity.

Maintenance

As your children become older you will have less control
over their diets. You may find (particularly if you have
been stingy on the sweet front) that they go overboard.
Give the freedom to do this, but warn them of the
consequences. It only takes one filling for children to sit
up and take note. When children start to demand or take
treats for granted, it's time to rethink your policy.

Talking Back

This is a funny one. We encourage our children to speak
their minds, to stand up for their own principles, to hold
their own ground and to negotiate and compromise. But
when they do it to us, we often call it talking back. And
that appears to be unacceptable. There is a fine line
between rudeness (disrespect) and stating a case or making

a point (respectful interaction). If your child can negotiate that fine line, you are going to have to learn to listen.

What to Do

1 Children should be encouraged to talk back as part of a conversation or regular communication. If you lash out at them for replying, you are going to stultify that relationship and make them uncertain and confused about exactly when it is appropriate to show all this independence you have been fostering.

2 That doesn't mean accepting rudeness or arguing. Insist upon a respectful tone of voice and choice of words, a reasoned argument and an appropriate time. For example, it's not OK for your children to resist an instruction and 'talk back' when you are in the middle of a conversation with someone else (interrupting), or when you have listened to their argument, considered their points and made a final decision. No means no.

3 Show respect for what they have to say when they present it respectfully. If they are being disdainful, patronizing or argumentative, you are within your rights to call an end to the conversation. Explain that you are willing to talk when they are willing to speak to you politely.

What Children Learn

That it is always appropriate to express themselves when it is undertaken with respect and courtesy. In this case it isn't 'talking back' but taking part in a conversation. They learn that they will always have a voice, but when you have considered the options and made a decision, you will stand by it.

Maintenance

If your child becomes 'lippy', you can always choose to ignore it. Say you are happy to talk if he can do it in a courteous manner, but that you don't think winding each other up or arguing is going to solve anything at all. He'll soon see you mean what you say and that negotiation only works when it is undertaken with the right intentions, and with a little charm.

Tantrums

Whole books have been devoted to this subject, and no one can ever seem to agree on the best strategy for dealing with this problem. The fact is that most children, and certainly all toddlers, throw tantrums. It's no reflection of your parenting skills; it's a behaviour that most children will experiment with from time to time. So what drives a child to tantrum? In younger children, it is simply an inability to express the overpowering emotions they are feeling – they may be angry, hurt, frustrated, lonely, bothered or simply fed up. They do not have the skills to work out what it is they are feeling; they just *act*. Older children throw tantrums for attention, or because it embarrasses or distresses their parents to the point where they always give in.

What to Do

1   The best way (which does take a lot of courage) is to ignore it completely. A child who gets no response by behaving in this type of uncontrolled way will soon see that he needs to adopt a better method. You are bound to get a lot of stick for ignoring a child, particularly in public places, but it is undoubtedly a technique that works. Some children have amazing tenacity and will continue long beyond the point

where you thought they would stop. But don't give in. Give in once and you've planted that all-important seed in his mind that he can use that technique again.

2   If it's too disruptive to allow a tantrum to continue, pick up your child, hug him tightly, say that you love him and then remove him from the scene. It might sound like rewarding problem behaviour by expressing love and affection, but your child may well feel out of control and need reassurance that everything is OK. The fact that his behaviour is not OK is something that will be discussed later. For the time being, you need to deal with the tantrum itself.

3   Offer choices: 'I can see you are very angry and upset. You can stop this behaviour now, we will finish our shopping and then have an ice cream. Or you can continue and we will have to leave now and go home with no treats.' Give them a little power to make a decision. Feeling powerless may well be one of the problems driving the tantrum.

4   Don't be tempted to negotiate with a child who is having a tantrum. He is unlikely to listen to reason and you'll probably only end up becoming angry, which is counterproductive. Negotiating is different to offering choices. When you offer choices you give options that have fixed results.

5   Be realistic about your expectations. If your child has been dragged around with you all day long, he's bound to be frazzled and exhausted. Don't expect perfect behaviour. Show some understanding and patience.

6   Talk to your children about feelings. Even small children can empathize to a certain extent. There are a number of good books that show children experiencing different emotions. Get some out of the library and use them as a talking point with your child.

7   Express understanding of the feeling they are experiencing, but make it clear that shows of temper are no way to deal with it. Ask them to think of better ways to show that they are angry, cross, tired or jealous.

8   Use yellow and red cards for warning and pre-arranged penalties (*see page 84*). Even small children will understand the concept. Yellow card means that this is your last warning. Red card means no video. Give them a warning. It might be enough to snap them out of the tantrum. If not, stick to your decision and award the penalty.

What Children Learn

They will see that violent or excessive behaviour is not going to get them what they want. They will learn that they can express their feelings in other ways, at which point you are always willing to listen and negotiate. They will see that you love them, regardless of how badly they behave on occasion. This helps them feel valued and important – key precursors to self-respect.

Maintenance

If the tantrums continue or start up again, bring up the problem at family meetings and get everyone involved in finding solutions, including your littlest members. Ask everyone what makes them feel like throwing a tantrum and what they do to control themselves. Your little one may appear uninterested, but he's likely to take on board the fact that everyone feels like exploding from time to time and that there are other ways to deal with it.

Telephones and Mobiles

Mobiles are the ultimate fashion accessory and certainly a key element in the way kids today communicate with each other. Having access to the telephone or their own mobile phone is important for kids because it gives them the freedom to communicate with their friends independently. It also makes them feel grown up, which is particularly important to teenagers, who are itching for the freedom that being 'grown up' offers. Problems crop up when telephones are overused, spending time that should be applied to other activities and schoolwork, and spending money.

What to Do

1   Children need to learn to respect the telephone. It costs money to use and is required for emergencies as well as for fun.

2   But respect, too, your child's need to communicate (sometimes for hours) with friends. Growing up is a difficult process and many children need constant reassurance, confirmation of their likeability and popularity, and regular interaction to get through it. Don't belittle that. I certainly remember spending more than my fair share of time on the telephone when I was growing up, and as far as I can see, it didn't cause any long-term damage.

3   Set limits in advance: 20 minutes maximum per call, maximum 3 calls per night. Bend the rules if there is something special going on or if your child seems distressed about something that she'd rather share with her friends. Make it clear from the outset, however, that you also need to use the phone and people need to be able to reach you.

4   If your child has a mobile, try to get a pay-as-you-go package so that she is in charge of funding her own calls (from pocket money or other sources). She'll learn moderation through necessity. Choose hours that her phone can be 'on' and insist that it stays off while she is doing homework or spending time with

the family. Mobiles can be enormously intrusive. The whole family should agree to this particular rule.

What Children Learn

To moderate their own behaviour in line with family expectations. To take financial responsibility for things that matter for them (which teaches them to prioritize and budget). To experience a little freedom and the joys of communication.

Television, Computers and Video Games

No child benefits from too much of any of these things. The problem is that many programmes and games can be inappropriate and/or violent, and chances are that you aren't there to limit the damage. Similarly, all of these things can be rather addictive and children get drawn into antisocial behaviour. Most importantly, however, they all represent distractions and this means that they are spending time in which they could be *interacting.* Remember, too, the health implications. If your child is sitting for hours in front of a screen, he's not being active. This will affect his heart, his weight and his overall mood.

What to Do

1   Limit television and computer games. If your children have extensive viewing habits, this will not be popular, but it's worth persevering. No child will benefit from inactivity, no matter how stubborn or determined he is to resist your attempts to make changes. Set an allocated period of time for each day, and relax the rules at the weekends. For example, you could suggest 30 minutes of television per day (they can choose their favourite programme) and 30 minutes on the computer. They can swap between the

two, if necessary. Don't worry about holidays and special occasions. If your child is getting lots of exercise and is outdoors for much of the time, a little longer in front of the television (watching a video or a film, for example) won't do as much harm as it will spending that long in front of a screen after a day behind a desk.

2   If you have a new computer or games console, now is the time to set down the rules: 'This has been allowed but we have reservations. We are prepared to allow you X number of minutes every day or at the weekend.' In our family, games consoles are banned during the week. This has never been a problem because it's always been the rule, and it's never even been questioned. Children who are busy with activities, interaction with their family, homework, reading and games will have little need to rely on what usually amounts to a solitary pursuit.

3   Ensure that your children are stimulated in other ways. Play games, talk, go on outings, read together, invite friends round. If there are other things in his life, he'll be less reliant on technology to keep him entertained.

4   Don't be tempted to use the television or computer as a baby-sitter. Your kids will develop a habit that is almost impossible to break.

5   Take the time to check out the games you buy. It may be that 'all their friends' have it, but if you don't think it's appropriate, explain why and don't buy it. There are plenty of other 'cool' games on the market. The same applies to television programmes. Don't ban games or programmes without explanation, but say that you don't think it's appropriate because of the swearing/sexual conduct/violence or whatever it is that worries you. But don't be unrealistic. Children

are, in today's society, in contact with a lot more than we ever were at that age. You can't wrap them in cotton wool. In the end, if they are going to be playing or watching it at every friend's home, you may have to see it as part of popular culture and relax your rules.

6   Whatever you do, avoid having the television on in the background. It's not only distracting, but it prevents real communication (everyone is only half listening) and positive interaction. It also teaches children that there has to be stimulation in the background at all times, when they'd do much better experiencing a little peace and relaxation.

7   At least an hour should elapse between watching television and going to bed to encourage optimum sleep. If your child has a favourite programme that comes on at a later hour, tape it and play it at a more appropriate time.

8   Quite apart from the effect that television has on sleep, it can take up time that could be spent reading, exercising or undertaking other healthy activities. Not all children are natural readers, but if they don't have the distraction of the television, they are more likely to pick up a book for entertainment.

9   Model the behaviour you want to see. If your sole form of relaxation is plopping in front of the box or surfing the internet, your kids are unlikely to see any real reason why they shouldn't too.

What Children Learn

That entertainment has a time and place, and that there are as many rewards and benefits to other activities. They also learn the art of moderation, and plan their time so that they can fit in everything they want to do.

Maintenance

You may need to refresh the rules from time to time. After holidays, for example, or illness, things can slip and the television may be on more than you'd like. Call a halt and begin again.

Telltale

Telltales are as frustrating for parents as they are for other children. It's a behaviour you will want to discourage as soon as possible. Children normally tell tales in an attempt to win favour, get attention, make themselves appear to be 'better' than their siblings or friends, or simply out of spite. None of these is a positive scenario. If your child regularly tells tales, it's a fairly good sign that she needs some more attention and her self-confidence and self-respect need a boost. She may feel she's constantly the underdog, or she may perceive inequality in the way you treat your children. She may well be wrong, but that's her perception and it's something you'll need to set right.

What to Do

1   Show a complete lack of interest when a child comes to you telling tales. Nod your head, say 'hmm' and carry on with whatever you are doing. If it's something serious, you may need to deal with it, but don't let on that their spying mission has had any real effect.

2   Show respect for her feelings. If she has come to you, she clearly has a problem that she is unable to solve or express. Give her the words to verbalize what she is thinking and help her solve the problem for herself. Show faith that she can do it.

3   Encourage respect between your children. It's healthy for them to have secrets from you and between

themselves. In fact, it solidifies the sibling relationship if your children are able to bond and trust one another. Respect their privacy, and do not be tempted to invade it on the say-so of a jealous, spiteful or attention-seeking child.

4   If you do need to intervene, take the opportunity, once again, to show faith in their ability to sort things out themselves. Say something along the lines of: 'I hear you have a problem. Why don't you stop this game and sit together on the sofa until you've worked it out?'

5   Take steps to boost self-respect (*see page 68*). Let your child know that you believe in her, that you love her as much as her siblings, that you trust her judgment and that you find her interesting/amusing/good company. Children often tell tales when they are feeling left out, so do what you can to include her in activities that make her feel good about herself.

What Children Learn

Children learn to solve problems without relying too heavily on you. While you have shown respect for their concerns, expressed understanding at the emotions they are feeling, as well as providing some advice and guidance, they do, in the end, learn that telling on others is no way to gain favour, deal with issues between siblings or friends or get your attention.

Maintenance

If your child reverts to telling tales, look at the reasons why this may be happening. Bring it up at your next family meeting and see if there is some discord within the family that could be addressed by a series of positive new goals. Remember that you need to find ways to recognize the problem without allowing your child to become overly reliant on your help. Continue to show faith in her ability to solve problems herself.

Toddlers

The year after your baby's first birthday marks the transition from babyhood to toddlerhood. By this time, life will have settled down into a recognizable routine that helps both you and your baby feel more confident about your relationship. This period bridges the gap between infancy and childhood, and your baby will be learning a great deal – particularly about being his own separate person – and is able to do more things for himself. These rapid changes will be both encouraging – as your baby becomes inquisitive and energetic, trying out new things and constantly testing himself, fired by an inspiring zest for life – and frustrating, as you will lock horns for the first time. His developing personality will be interspersed with periods of rest, or regression back to babyish ways. He will need the comfort of familiar routines, games and cuddles, as he learns more and struggles to meet the demands of the world around him.

Until now, your baby has been totally dependent upon you, his parents, for his every need. You have been his favourite people, and may have felt both flattered and enslaved by his focus and dependence on you. By the time his first birthday comes around, however, this situation is slowly changing. Your baby will now have a firm grip on life, the result of your constant care during the first year, and he will be consumed with the task of growing up. By now, well established as part of the family, he will widen his horizons to encompass other family members apart from his mother and father. This period is unique in that he will develop physically at a tremendous rate – learning to crawl, if he hasn't already done so, walk and then run. He will delight in activity and be into everything with enthusiasm and unending curiosity. His determination to learn everything he can about his environment and the world around him means that he will be capable of disappearing without a moment's notice or creating chaos in a room in just a few minutes. This focus and drive may fill you with pride and amusement one minute – and exasperation the next.

The difficulties of this period are compounded by your baby's single-minded resolve to do exactly as he pleases – but he will require the comfort of the knowledge that you are there when he needs you, and you will certainly hear about it when you are not. He will shun your attempts to help him because he will be confident that he is capable of doing everything for himself – from changing his own nappies to feeding himself, from carrying the groceries to building his own block towers. He won't understand danger and you will need to intervene constantly to ensure his safety, and to pick up the pieces when he dissolves into tears of frustration.

Toddlers can't control their emotions or understand the concept of 'later'. They think in terms of the here-and-now, and he will battle determinedly for what he wants, even in the face of your obvious displeasure. Most toddlers are not deliberately naughty – they genuinely forget what they have been told, or attribute little significance to it. Your toddler will not yet be able to discern between what is acceptable and what is considered naughty, and if the inspiration strikes him, he will do exactly as he pleases. His overwhelming curiosity may drive you to distraction. Some people call this period the 'Terrible Twos' and, for many babies, with good reason.

Don't be too heavy with discipline. Your toddler will be exploring his world and needs to learn to see the positive, rather than all the things he cannot do. But be firm. Don't allow your toddler to exert his new-found authority and independence in inappropriate ways. He'll understandably need to know what is expected of him, what is allowed and what is not. But he may think he's a step ahead of you, and he'll use everything in his repertoire – including tantrums and emotional blackmail – to get his own way. Be patient, loving, but firm. Teach through example. Explain as much as you can. Teach him words to understand what he is feeling and show him that other people feel the same way. Show him the impact his behaviour has on others. In this way he will begin to understand the concept of taking responsibility for actions and the need for respect.

Respect his individuality and his unique perspective of life, as well as his personality. If he grows up feeling good about himself, his emotional foundation will be strong enough to resist all sorts of challenges and he will learn to be confident about being himself.

However trying he might be, your toddler will be enormously rewarding and will make you helpless with laughter. You will share his pride in new achievements – from learning to walk, to feeding himself, from possibly making his first steps towards potty-training, to speaking his first clear words and even sentences with purpose. Try to take pleasure in his boundless enthusiasm and delight, and show your approval whenever you can. He will move forward with great confidence into childhood.

Travelling in the Car

No one likes sitting in the car for long periods of time. For children, it can seem interminable, particularly if they have a sibling next to them winding them up. Holidays and even short trips can be ruined if your children fight and whine throughout the journey, so it's important to ensure they are given the opportunity to let off a little steam from time to time, and that you keep them occupied.

What to Do

1 Plan your journey with plenty of pit stops to let the kids out to run. Most service stations have playgrounds, make use of them.

2 Tell them in advance exactly what to expect: when and where you will be stopping, how long it will take to get there, what you will be having for lunch and what to expect when you get there. Although even the best-laid plans can go awry, if the children have an idea of what to expect, they'll be far more patient.

3   Bring along story tapes, laptop games and snacks to
    punctuate the journey. Allow each child to choose a
    game and get everyone involved in playing. If your
    children are older, allow them to choose a CD, tape or
    radio station for a set period of time, and plan this in
    advance to prevent the ubiquitous battle.

4   Swap their seats at every pit stop to ensure that
    everyone feels they have had their turn at the
    window or on the side of the car they wish to be.
    Sounds silly, but these are the type of things that
    wind children up.

5   Be prepared for outlandish behaviour. On one car
    journey with my children, one of my sons actually
    complained that the other was 'looking out of *his*
    window'. Beat that.

6 Don't push it until everyone is tired and grumpy.
   Stop early enough so that you can have some space
   away from each other and time to unwind.
7 Get the children to pack a journey bag with special
   toys, treats, cameras, games and anything else that
   will keep them occupied.

What Children Learn

Children learn patience! Travelling can be frustrating for
all involved, but if they learn that a positive attitude and a
willingness to while away the hours without fuss keep
things on an even keel, they'll be more likely to repeat that
behaviour.

Up and Out in the Morning

Morning is one of the most difficult times of the day and
often the source of a great deal of family disharmony and
arguments. There are several reasons for problems here.
The main one is that few of us are at our best in the
morning and would much rather be in bed than nudging a
sleepy, stubborn child out of bed, to the breakfast table,
bathroom and out the front door – with everything she is
expected to have. Some children count on this as an
opportunity to wind you up and get a little attention, and
they are right. It's an activity that has to happen, and you
will end up as part of the scrum if you don't set down
some rules and routines – and fast.

What to Do

1 Make things easy on yourself. Set out uniforms or
   school clothing the night before. Make the packed
   lunches and pop them in the fridge. Get all the
   school bags by the door as well as the required
   coats, shoes, hats and umbrellas. If you have time,

set the breakfast table the night before. Anything
that takes the pressure off the morning battle
will help. Better still, give each child a checklist
and get them to take part in the pre-morning
organization.

2   Give your child plenty of time to wake properly.
Rushing children up and out of the door is bound to
fray tempers, unless you have super-speedy kids who
don't mind doing things at top gear.

3   If there is a choice of clothing required in the
morning, ask your child to make it the night before
and get it all laid out. She may change her mind in
the morning, but chances are she'll remember she
made a decision and go with it.

4   Don't be overambitious with breakfast. If your
children have a wholesome cold meal – cereal, fruit
and juice – they'll get on just fine. Don't make a rod
for your own back. Give them some choices (of cereal,
for example, or of toppings for their toast) to avoid an
inevitable argument over serving the 'wrong'
breakfast. Make the choices necessarily limited. As
long as they have some power over what they are
served, they'll be more likely to accept it.

5   Make the morning routine absolutely rigid. If the
same things happen at the same time every day, your
children will eventually just go with the flow.

6   Avoid distractions at all cost. If that television is
turned on, for example, you are very unlikely to be
able to shift them until there is a commercial break or
the programme finishes. Make it taboo in the
morning. It may sound tough, but it's much easier in
the long run to ban something completely than it is to
negotiate when the clock is ticking.

7   Get your child her own alarm clock. Set it for five
minutes before you plan to wake her yourself. When

you do go in to see that she's up, you will hopefully have missed the first morning grouchiness.

8   If you have early risers, encourage them to get dressed on their own and play games together, or read a book. Again, don't be tempted to allow the television or games console to be used to keep them occupied.

What Children Learn

The art of organization! Everyone can see that it's much easier to get up and out if things are organized in advance. They also learn that a day that starts on the right foot is better for everyone involved.

Maintenance

Keep the routine in place as much as possible. There are always times when things slip, but if you work on pre-organization, on encouraging your children to take responsibility for their belongings and deciding in advance what will be required, you are likely to have a much easier run. If the mornings are still problematic, bring them up at family meetings and ask your children how they think things can work more smoothly. No one wants to head off to a job or school with an argument ringing in their ears. If you do succumb to a collision with your child, make sure you make amends before she leaves the front door, or your car.

Violence

Violence is the physical manifestation of anger and aggression, and it's something that needs to be curbed at whatever cost. Early on, many parents send conflicting messages to children regarding violence, by succumbing to smacking or expressing their fury through violent actions, such as kicking or throwing something across the room.

I'm not saying that all parents do this, but children learn what they live, and if they see violence in their everyday life, they are bound to repeat it.

Another problem is, of course, the fact that children are witness to violence on television, computer games, games consoles and a variety of other sources. In fact, by the time they reach the age of about 11, the average child will have witnessed more than 100 thousand acts of violence on television. Children may be exposed to as many as five violent acts per hour during prime time and an average of 26 violent acts per hour during Saturday morning children's programmes.

Combine this with the fact that children who cannot express themselves verbally, or find it difficult to find an outlet for their frustration, naturally use their bodies as a form of expression, and you have trouble waiting to happen.

What to Do

1   Ensure your child is not regularly viewing material unsuitable for his age. If you can, watch or play with him to explain what is unacceptable.

2   Look at your family situation and ensure there is no violence being witnessed by your child. Is your relationship with your partner one of conflict? It may be that your children are taking on board the problems and acting them out physically.

3   Hold regular family meetings to get the message across that violence is taboo (*see page 33*). Violence against others or destruction of property will never be tolerated, and this is one case where a warning may not even be necessary.

4   Teach your child alternative methods of expressing himself – get a punchbag if you need to. If you have a physical child who finds it easiest to let off steam by

doing something active, then find a way for this to happen.

5 Practise what you preach. Smacking or any other form of violence should be banned from the home.

6 Talk about the way your child is feeling, and give him the words to express himself. If he can get out the rage in other ways, he'll be less likely to lash out.

What Children Learn

Everyone has a propensity to be violent and if we did not learn control, our society would be in even more of a mess than it is now. The fact is that all children need to learn that violence – against anyone or anything – is completely unacceptable. Make it a moral lesson and drive it home as often as you need to. Children can learn to let off their frustration and anger in other ways, and if you guide them through the process, they will.

Parenting Sites On-line

There are a multitude of good websites catering for parents facing various problems and issues with their children. Although some of the advice can be conflicting, and therefore confusing, many of these sites offer tips and stories from parents themselves. Remember: stick with the techniques offered in this book, and adapt them to fit your individual scenario. If you are still facing difficulties, look at some of the parenting sites online, or contact me on Childhealt@aol.com.

Parenthood.com is a good site, with a wealth of information on all aspects of bringing up children.
Website: www.parenthood.com

Childline is a great website aimed at children facing various problems. Worth a look for parents, too, as it deals with many crucial issues such as bullying and peer pressure.
Website: www.childline.org.uk

NCH Action for Children produces expert online and printed resources for children, young people, parents and social work practitioners and policy makers.
Website: www.nchafc.org.uk

NSPCC runs a fantastic website with advice for parents and children alike on all of the main issues, including a special section on bullying.
Website: www.nspcc.org.uk
Website: www.bullying.co.uk

Young Minds promote the mental health and emotional well-being of children and young people. Also has a helpline and information aimed at parents.
Website: www.youngminds.org.uk

Babyworld offers advice for parents of small children – how to set them on the right course and deal with problems as they crop up. Good section on the importance of routine.
Website: www.babyworld.com

Kidshealth looks at more than just physical health issues, with good sections on positive parenting, as well as emotions and behaviour.
Website: www.kidshealth.org

Parentsoup is a vast website with information on all aspects of parenting, including discipline, emotional health, sleep problems and much, much more. Worth a look.
Website: www.parentsoup.com

National Family and Parenting Institute is an independent charity working to improve the lives of parents and families by campaigning for a more family-friendly society. Plenty of good advice and information.
Website: www.e-parents.org

Nurturing magazine site is a good 'natural parenting' website.
Website: www.nurturing.ca/home

This Canadian site has links to more than 5,500 health and 'wellness' sites on the web. Over half of these are rated and reviewed. Plenty of advice for parents on emotional health issues that might be underpinning discipline problems.
Website: www.bc.sympatico.ca/Contents/health/

What to Do When You Can't Keep the Peace: Extra Help and What's Available

Don't hesitate to ask for expert help when things spiral out of control. There are a wealth of support agencies and charities set up to help parents facing difficult periods. Most offer helplines and support groups, and will deal with problems sensitively and in confidence.

Some children suffer from stress, emotional problems and other issues that send them beyond the normal, unpleasant symptoms and feelings. There are many natural and practical solutions to many of these issues, as outlined in this book, but there may be times when a child's health, development and well-being are severely threatened. At this point, they may need drug therapy and/or counselling or psychiatric help. There is no need to be ashamed if your child requires this type of assistance. In the long term, a short period turned over to this type of intervention can make a difference to your child's future ability to adapt to the world around him, and to find health and happiness as an adult.

It's also important for parents to understand that a child's inability to cope with the rigours of modern life is no reflection on parenting skills or a child's future capability and success. It is abundantly clear that the stress of modern life is taking its toll on even the most robust of us, and children are no exception.

There may be times, too, when you need a little extra support. Parenting is a difficult job, and none of us can be completely prepared for every eventuality. If you find that you are out of your depth and finding yourself unable to cope, don't hesitate to consider expert advice. There are numerous helplines set up for parents, and it may well be that family therapy or counselling could sort out issues that simply don't respond to common sense advice.

The following organisations may be able to help:

International Stress Management Association (ISMA)
PO Box 348
Waltham Cross
EN8 8ZL
Tel: 07000 780430
Fax: +44 (0) 1992 426673
E-mail: stress@isma.org.uk
Website: www.isma.org.uk
Stress is often a precursor to family problems, and this organisation offers a host of informative articles and ways of dealing with stress in people of all ages.

UK Council for Psychotherapy
167–169 Great Portland Street
London
W1N 5PB
Tel: 020 7436 3002 (Mon–Fri: 9am–5pm)
Website: www.psychotherapy.org.uk
This organisation is responsible for promoting high standards in the field of psychotherapy, and can help to put you in touch with a reputable, registered psycho-therapist. Many families benefit from family therapy during difficult periods, and an unbiased expert can often help to pinpoint fundamental problems that may have been overlooked. Never be embarrassed about seeking extra help.

NSPCC
42 Curtain Road
London
EC2A 3NH
Tel: 020 7825 2500
Fax: 020 7825 2525
Helpline: 0808 800 5000 (Freephone 24 hours)

Textphone: 0800 056 0566
Website: www.nspcc.org.uk
Website: www.bullying.co.uk
A great organisation helping parents and children alike with all of the most common problems facing parents and kids of today. They are happy to take calls or emails on the numbers above, and can advise on support groups also.

Gingerbread
Advice line: 0800 018 4318 (Mon–Fri: 9am–5pm)
Website: www.gingerbread.org.uk
Gingerbread is the leading support organisation for lone parent families in England and Wales.

Parentline Plus
Helpline: 0808 800 2222
Website: www.parentlineplus.org.uk
A UK-registered charity which offers support to anyone parenting a child – the child's parents, step-parents, grandparents and foster parents. Parentline Plus runs a freephone helpline, courses for parents, develops innovative projects and provides a range of information. Their website has a huge number of topical issues with advice.

The Samaritans
Tel: 08457 90 90 90 (cost of a local call)
Tel: 1850 60 90 90 (Republic of Ireland)
E-mail: jo@samaritans.org
Website: www.samaritans.org.uk
Offers a confidential listening and e-mail service 24 hours a day.

ChildLine
2nd Floor
Royal Mail Building
Studd Street
London
N1 0QW
Tel: 020 7239 1000
Helpline: 0800 1111 (24 hours a day)
Fax: 020 7239 1001
Website: www.childline.org.uk
If your child needs to talk and you aren't able to get through to him or her, they may find some comfort talking things over with one of Childline's trained professionals.